Black
and White
Mixed
Marriages

Black and White Mixed Marriages

Ernest Porterfield

Nelson-Hall/Chicago

To Jean, Jeffrey, Jerald, and Jerome

Library of Congress in Publication Data

Porterfield, Ernest.
  Black and white mixed marriages.

    Bibliography: p. 173
    Includes index.
      1. Interracial marriage—United States—Case
studies. I. Title.
HQ1031.P64   301.42′9′0973   77-8796
ISBN 0-88229-131-9 (cloth)
ISBN 0-88229-484-9 (paper)

contents

tables

preface

BLACK-WHITE MARRIAGES in the United States have long been a subject little talked about and, for various reasons, one of limited sociological inquiry. Surprisingly, there are few studies regarding this subject. And most of these are out of date. It is partly this tradition that stimulated me to undertake research regarding this complex and gradually growing phenomenon. Since one would naturally expect the black-white marriage pattern to take on new dimensions after the passage of the civil rights legislation of 1964 and 1965, as well as the 1967 United States Supreme Court's decision declaring miscegenation laws to be unconstitutional, and since most of the literature on this topic predates that legislation, I thought it worth my efforts to investigate this area.

In spite of a vast and growing amount of interest in this marital combination, knowledge of its nature, extent, and changing character is quite inadequate. Information from marriage and divorce records is fragmentary and inaccurate for a variety of reasons. Registration and publication of statistics have been deficient; and currently, there is a trend toward removal of racial identification from public records. And even when available, in some areas, the publication of such is prohibited by law.

This study presents a systematic ethnographic description of forty black-white families. If focuses attention on intrafamilial relations, interactional patterns between families and their kin network, and relations between these unions and larger society. A secondary aim is to generate greater understanding of the possibilities of, as well as the difficulties in, developing an egalitarian multiracial society (such as the United States) through large-scale miscegenation.

Despite the persistence of negative attitudes and reactions toward black-white marriage, a small number of blacks and whites continue to intermarry. In light of recent social, economic, and political changes, a number of important questions are now being raised about these alliances. First, this book examines perspectives on black-white intermixture in colonial America. It then traces the incidence of and summarizes research findings on black-white marriages from 1897-1964. A description of methodological procedures in conducting this research follows. Other topics discussed are motives for intermarriage; marriage between black men/white women and white men/black women; dating, marriage and intrafamilial and interfamilial relations; interactional patterns with larger society; and egalitarianism through black nationalism.

A considerable number of people provided much assistance in the undertaking of this project. First, I would like to acknowledge my debt to the black-white families who made this study possible and to Paul J. Cooper, Jr., for introducing me to and arranging interviews for the Cambridge, Ohio sample. Pseudonyms are used throughout to protect the anonymity of these families. Their cooperation, openness, and patience are immeasurable.

Abundant gratitude is offered to Professor Bernard Farber (Arizona State University) who chaired my dissertation committee and further stimulated and supported my interest in family sociology from the beginning of my graduate career at the University of Illinois. He provided unceasing guidance, as well as intellectual and emotional support during my stay at the university. I would like to thank Professor William C. Jenné (Oregon State University) for his encouragement, and prompt and persistent readings and critical comments on earlier drafts of the manuscript. Special recognition is accorded Professor J. E. Hulett, Jr., (University of Illinois) and Jan Brukman (Beloit College) for their valuable suggestions, guidance, and discussions of earlier drafts of this report. I also owe special thanks to Dr. George E. Passey, Dean of the School of Social and Behavioral Sciences (University of Alabama in Birmingham) for a reduction in teaching load during 1976, which allowed me to devote more time to the study. I am grateful for partial financial support from the University of Alabama Research Grant Committee.

For the patient and efficient typing of several early drafts of the manuscript, I am grateful to Judy Broom. Special thanks go to Linda Kicker and Marilyn Southern for typing the final draft. Gratitude is also accorded Vicky Savage, for preparing the index; LeVorian Stephens for consultation and editing; and Patricia Reedy, Sharon Maley, and Patrick Hanrahan for transcribing some of the taped interviews.

acknowledgments

I WISH TO thank the following authors and/or publishers of copyrighted materials for permission to adapt or reprint their work:

C. H. Anderson, *Toward A New Sociology: A Critical View* (Homewood, Ill.: Dorsey Press, 1971), pp. 83-85, 88-89. Reprinted with permission.

Lerone Bennett, Jr., *Before the Mayflower: A History of Black America* (Chicago: Johnson Publishing, 1969), pp. 244, 249-251, 255-258, 263, by permission of the publisher.

Elridge Cleaver, *Soul On Ice* (New York: Dell, 1968), p. 14. Used with permission of McGraw-Hill Publishing Company

Carl N. Degler, *Neither Black Nor White* (New York: Macmillan, 1971). Copyright ©1971, Carl N. Degler, by permission of the publisher.

St. Clair Drake and Horace Cayton, *Black Metropolis* (New York: Harcourt Brace Jovanovich, 1945), pp. 133, 138-141, 154-159, by permission of the publisher.

W.E.B. Dubois, *The Philadelphia Negro: A Social Study* (New York: Schocken, 1967), pp. 358–367, by permission of the publisher.

Bernard Farber, *Comparative Kinship Systems* (New

York: John Wiley and Sons, 1968), p. 10, by permission of the author and publisher.

From Chapter 1, of *Kinship and Class: A Midwestern Study*, by Bernard Farber, ©1971 by Basic Books, New York.

Bernard Farber, *Family: Organization and Interaction* (San Francisco: Chandler, 1964), pp. 105, 122, by permission of author and publisher.

From *Minorities, Civil Rights, and Protest*, by Charles W. Fisher, p. 19. Copyright ©1970 by Dickenson Publishing Co. Encino, California. Reprinted by permission of the publisher.

Robin Fox, *Kinship and Marriage* (Baltimore: Pelican Original—Penguin Books Ltd., 1967). Copyright ©Robin Fox, 1967, pp. 228, 235, 238-239, by permission of the publisher.

Noel P. Gist and Sylvia F. Fava, *Urban Society* (New York: Thomas Y. Crowell, 1974), pp. 330-331. Copyright 1974, 1964, 1956, 1948, 1941 (renewed 1969 by Gist and Halbert), 1933 (renewed by Mary L. Halbert and Noel P. Gist) by Thomas Y. Crowell Co., by permission of the publisher.

William H. Grier and Price M. Cobbs, *Black Rage* (New York: Basic Books, 1968), p. 92, by permission of the publisher.

Richard H. Klemer, *Marriage and Family Relationships* (New York: Harper and Row, 1970), pp. 110–112. Copyright ©1970 by Richard H. Klemer, by permission of the publisher.

Cloyte M. Larsson, *Marriage Across the Color Line* (Chicago: Johnson Publishing Company, 1965), pp. 37, 38, 55-57, 60, by permission of the publisher.

Robert K. Merton, "Intermarriage and the Social Structure: Fact and Theory," *Psychiatry* 4 (August 1941): 361–374, in Rose L. Coser, ed. *The Family: Its Structure and Functions* (New York: St. Martin's, 1964), p. 128. Copyright held by William Alanson White Psychiatric Foundation. Reprinted by permission of the author and publisher.

Edward B. Reuter, *Race Mixture: Studies in Intermarriage and Miscegenation* (New York: McGraw-Hill, 1931), pp. 27-30, 78-82, 98, 99, 101, 103. Copyright ©1931, McGraw-Hill, by permission of the publisher.

Lloyd Saxton, *The Individual, Marriage, and the Family* (Belmont, California: Wadsworth, 1968), p. 330, by permission of the publisher.

Robert Staples, "The Myth of the Black Matriarchy," in Robert Staples, ed. *The Black Family: Essays and Studies* (Belmont, Calif.: Wadsworth, 1971), pp. 150-151. Reprinted by permission of *The Black Scholar*.

Robert S. Stuckert, "The African Ancestry of the White American Population," *Ohio Journal of Science*, 58 (May 1958): 155-160, by permission of the publisher.

Pierre L. Van den Berghe, *Race and Racism: A Comparative Perspective* (New York: John Wiley and Sons, 1967), pp. 42-60, by permission of the publisher.

Louis Wirth and Herbert Goldhamer, "The Hybrid and the Problem of Miscegenation," in Otto Klineberg, ed. *Characteristics of the American Negro* (New York: Harper and Row, 1944), pp. 249-370. Copyright 1944 by Harper and Rows, by permission of the publisher.

Perspectives on Black-White Intermixture

THE EARLY ENGLISH settlers in North America, unlike many of their European counterparts from Spain and Portugal who settled in Mexico and Brazil, soon became extremely averse to racial amalgamation. One of the primary reasons for the development of this ideological system appeared not to have been sex but instead social legitimacy and status positions. For example, in a society stratified by race rather than lineage, the chastity of women of the dominant race must be guarded with great care—which in effect means that these women are not to cohabit with men of subordinate racial or ethnic groups. Such intercaste sexual relations between "superiors" and "inferiors" would certainly undermine the power base of the "superiors."

One only has to take a panoramic view of the spectrum of race relations to easily detect that cross-racial sex is one of the most virulent and latently emotional foundations which supports the United States castelike system. When a male of a minority group openly attempts to assert his manhood by competing for tabooed women, larger society often reacts with a display of fear, hostility, and sometimes violence. The range of emotions reflects the ambivalence that exists in this country toward black-white couples. Much of this behavior results in sexual paranoia on the part of both blacks and whites.

Much of the mysticism and confusion surrounding interracial sexual relations in the United States can be traced to the unique conditions of slavery. In an effort to explore this idea, this chapter has two objectives. First, it examines the nature of the social, sexual, and marital relationships between blacks and whites in the early settlement of this country. This examination includes a description of demographic, legal, and social trends—emphasizing reasons for miscegenation laws, and how such laws were passed by various states in an attempt to deter marriage between blacks and whites. Second, it introduces some theoretical frames of reference which will guide this investigation.

MISCEGENATION IN EARLY AMERICA

Whether by original nature or in response to the requirement of continued existence, man has always been a restless animal. The inevitable result of migration is new human contact and group and culture conflict. The initial conflict eventually gives way to some sort of working relationship and is ultimately resolved in a mutual accommodation to a blended culture. An incidental but frequent outcome of human contact and association is the mixture of different racial stocks and the fusion of ethnic types through interbreeding. While the mixture of races is old and widespread, it is chiefly within recent periods that this has given rise to political and sociological problems.[1]

Socioeconomic conditions in the early American colonies encouraged racial mingling. White men and women from England, Ireland, and Scotland were bought and sold in the same markets with black men and women and bequeathed in the same wills. They were subjected to similar working and living conditions after their arrival in America. As indentured servants bound out for five or seven years, whites worked in the same fields with black servants and lived in the same rude tenant huts. A deep bond of sympathy developed between these indentured servants and blacks who formed the bulk of the early population. They fraternized during off-duty hours and consoled themselves with the same strong rum. And in and out of wedlock, they produced a numerous mulatto brood.[2]

The Rate of Intermixture

The actual statistics of race intermixture in the United States are of the most meager sort, and those available are not always wholly dependable. The only general statistics are those of the federal censuses of 1850, 1860, 1870, 1890, and 1910. No other general census made a distinction in the returns between the full-blood and the mixed-blood Negroes. Prior to 1850— that is, for four-fifths of the period that the Negro has been in America—there are only occasional estimates and partial statistical reports of sections, states, or cities made for special purposes.[3]

The term *mulatto* is used throughout this book to designate the offspring of a Negro and a white parent; in a more general sense, a person of mixed Caucasian and Negro blood, or Indian and Negro blood. The *Mulatto*, as the concept was used in the early history of this country, includes all those members of the Negro race with a visible admixture of white blood. Thus used, the word is a general term to include all Negroes of mixed ancestry regardless of the degree of intermixture. It includes all persons who are recognized, in the communities in which they live, as being of mixed blood. The United States Census Office has not been consistent in its definition of the term. "The fact that the definition of the term 'mulatto' adopted at different censuses has not been entirely uniform may in some degree affect the comparability of the figures." In 1870 and 1910, however, the term was applied to all persons having any perceptible trace of Negro blood, excepting, of course, Negroes of pure blood. In 1850 and 1860, the term seems not to have been defined. In the returns for 1890 the Negroes of mixed blood were classified as mulattos, quadroons, and octoroons.[4] Table 1-1 reports the Negro population for the Continental United States from 1850–1910.

Table 1-1
Continental United States Negro Population

Census Year	Total Negro	Black	Mulatto	Percent Mulatto
1850	3,638,808	3,233,057	405,751	11.2
1860	4,441,830	3,853,467	588,363	13.2
1870	4,880,009	4,295,960	584,049	12.0
1890	7,488,676*	6,337,980	1,132,060	15.2
1910	9,827,763	7,777,077	2,050,686	20.9

*This figure includes 18,636 Negroes enumerated in Indian Territory not distinguished as black or mulatto.
Source: Edward B. Reuter, *The Mulatto in the United States* (Boston: Gorham Press, 1918), p. 118.

The censuses of mulattoes, as distinguished from full-blooded Negroes, taken in 1850, 1860, 1870, and 1890, though subject to a far greater and wholly indeterminate probable error, have shown a general agreement of results.[5] The United States Census count in 1920 was the last year a distinction was made between mulato and black.[6] Figure 1 provides a genealogical description of three categories of racial admixtures commonly referred to in the United States as the mulatto, quadroon, and octoroon.

One of the results of marital and extramarital miscegenation is the appearance of a number of persons who cannot be distinguished physically from members of the majority group. Such individuals may or may not *pass* for white.[7] There are no accurate figures on the extent of *passing* which occurs in the United States. Estimates of those who leave the Negro group permanently and are absorbed by white society vary from a few thousands to tens of thousands annually.

By *passing* is meant the successful and permanent assumption of white status by a person who knows he has Negro an-

Figure 1. Genealoigcal Illustration of Three Categories of Racial Admixtures

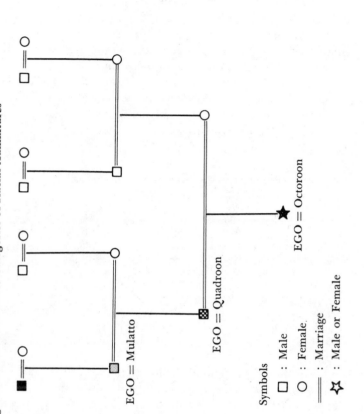

EGO. The person whose viewpoint is used to describe genealogical relationships in a kinship system.

Mulatto. A person one of whose parents is black and the other white. The individual is said to be "one-half black and one-half white."

Quadroon. The child of a mulatto and a white person. A person who has one black grandparent. A quadroon is "one-fourth black."

Octoroon. Offspring of a quadroon and a white. A person with one black and seven white grandparents. An octoroon is "one-eighth black."

Symbols

□ : Male
○ : Female.
═ : Marriage
☆ : Male or Female

EGO = Mulatto

EGO = Quadroon

EGO = Octoroon

cestry.[8] Stuckert, using the method of genetic probability tables, estimates the number of blacks who passed during the period 1861-1960. The main finding of his study was that 28 million white persons have some African ancestry. Another way of putting it is that in 1960, 77.4 percent of the black population of the United States had some degree of non-African ancestry.[9] A summary of this data is reported in Table 1-2.

Table 1-2
Estimates on the Number of Persons Passing

Decades	Number Passing
1861–1890	90,900
1891–1910	103,300
1911–1930	183,200
1931–1940	42,700
1941–1950	155,500
1951–1960	96,900

Source: Robert S. Stuckert, "The African Ancestry of the White American Population," *Ohio Journal of Science*, 55 (May 1958); 155-160.

We should be reminded, however, that individuals who pass do not always do so in an attempt to lose their identity. There are several reasons for passing. Some are: (1) passing intentionally; (2) passing for convenience; (3) passing for fun; and (4) passing for economic necessity or advantage.[10] I might also add that many persons pass unintentionally—i.e., they are perceived by the larger community to be white.

Social Class and Racial Crossing

Intermingling among the lower classes was quite common. On the other hand, it was not altogether absent from the upper classes. Concubinage in most Southern cities was a luxury of the idle rich. In New Orleans, Charleston, and several other cities, there were organized systems of concubinage. Needless to say, some of the most prominent men of the South patronized the system. It was widely said and believed in the slave period that Thomas Jefferson (1743-1826) had slave mistresses and slave children. According to reports, his favorite mistress was Black Sal who was fair-skinned with long hair and Caucasian features. Pearl M. Graham wrote: "By the time Jefferson turned the reins of government over to James Madison in 1809, Sally was the busy mother of several younglings who closely resembled Jefferson."

In September 1948, W. Edward Farrison (a professor), interviewed three sisters "who were obviously far from being full-blooded Negroes, each of whom was more than sixty-five years of age, and who traced their lineage directly to Sally Hemings through her daughter Harriet, who was born in May 1801, and whose father those sisters had been told was Thomas Jefferson."

From a study of contemporary and modern sources, Ms. Graham has proved, to her satisfaction anyway, that Sally Hemings bore Jefferson "at least four children, possibly six." The children under the name of Sally Hemings listed in Jefferson's Farm Book, were:

Hemings, Sally, 1773
    Beverly, 1798
    Harriet, May 1801
    Madison, January 1805
    Eston, May 1808

Jefferson was not the only famous American to wander across the color line. Patrick Henry (1736-1799) reportedly fathered a black son, Melancthon. According to persistent reports, Alexander Hamilton (1757-1804), who was born in the West Indies, had some black blood. "If Hamilton was not a Negro," Professor Maurice R. Davie wrote, "he certainly brought two Negro sons into the world." Another case in point is that of William Wells Brown, the black abolitionist. Rumor had it that his mother was a daughter of Daniel Boone (1734-1820).

Benjamin Franklin (1700-1790), it is said by the historian, Carter Woodson, "seems to have made no secret of his association with Negro women." It was also rumored that George Washington (1732-1799) fathered mulatto children. Well-to-do-people, however, usually stopped short of marriage.

Several well-known mulattoes were products of unions between blacks and whites. Lemmel Haynes, a New Englander, who later married a white woman, Bessie Babbit, was probably the first Negro to preach regularly to a white congregation. Benjamin Banneker, the astronomer and mathematician, was the grandson of Molly Welch, an interesting Englishwoman who came to Maryland as an indentured servant. Robert Purvis, the brilliant black abolitionist, was one of many mulattoes shipped North by penitent white fathers. So fair that he could have passed for white, Purvis refused to abandon his mother's people and made an important contribution in the antislavery fight. James Augustine Healy, the first Negro Roman Catholic priest in America, and the first Negro American to become a Catholic bishop, was also a mulatto. Others would include persons like Frederick Douglass, Booker T. Washington, W. E. B. Dubois.

In some cases, plantation amalgamation was the result of what A. W. Calhoun called "the master's right of rape." Threats, promises, the whip, and the lash were used to subvert the morals of slave women. But force was not always necessary. The superior prestige and power of white men captivated some slave women. Mutual attraction played a part in the other relationships. An additional factor was the indefensible position of a whole class of women whose only weapons were sexual. Some slave women apparently enjoyed the give-and-take of liaison, which involved direct and open competition with white women.

White women were also a factor in American amalgamation in the plantation period. According to Kenneth Stamp, white women were less involved in amalgamation than white men but their role "was never negligible." James Hugo Johnston observed also that white women are partially responsible for the existence of American mulattoes.[11]

Antimiscegenation Laws

In the beginning little social distinction was made in America on the basis of race. However, as the racial justification for slavery developed, there began to creep into the mores a distinction between Negroes and whites. One of its first manifestations was the passage of laws against intermarriage.[12] When black servants were reduced to slavery, the colonial governing classes redoubled their efforts to stamp out racial mixing. Miscegenation in this era was not only a serious breach of Puritan morality, but also a serious threat to slavery and the stability of the servile labor force.[13]

The earliest record available against the cohabitation of black-white servants was the case of Hugh Davis, a white servant in Virginia who was sentenced to a public beating on September 17, 1630, "before an assembly of negroes and others" for "defiling himself with a Negro. . . . It was required that he confess as much the following Sabbath."

The first law to deter racial intermarriage was enacted in the early colonial period. The General Assembly of the Colony of Maryland in 1661 deplored the fact that there were many cases of intermarriage between white female servants and Negro slaves. The question arose as to the status of white servants and their children by Negro men. It legislated that if any free born white woman intermarried with a Negro slave, she would have to serve her husband's master as long as the slave lived. Children of all these marriages would also be slaves. Children of racial intermarriages which occurred before the law was passed were to remain with their parents' master until they were thirty years of age. In 1681 a new Maryland law decreed that any freeborn white woman who married a Negro slave with the permission of the slave's master could retain her freedom. Her children were also free. However, the master or mistress of the intermarried slave and the clergyman performing the ceremony were to be penalized by a fine. This law was an attempt to deter racial intermarriage by shifting the penalty to those allegedly responsible for the action of slaves.

Some of the other colonies also legislated against Negro-white intermarriage. North Carolina in 1715 set up a heavy fine and a period of servitude for any white who married a Negro. It also provided a fifty-pound fine for the clergyman who officiated. Massachusetts in 1705 and Pennsylvania in 1725 passed similar legislation.

In the legislatures of several of the states which had no prohibitive laws, bills to prevent Negro-white marriages were introduced—in some cases several times. They were Wisconsin, Massachusetts, Connecticut, Washington, Kansas, Minnesota, Iowa, Illinois, Michigan, Ohio, Pennsylvania, and New York. Congress had also considered bills to prevent racial intermarriage in the District of Columbia. The states which had laws followed a general regional pattern. All Southern states, as well as most Western states, had laws against Negro-white intermarriage.

After the United States became a nation, eventually thirty-three states (the majority being Southern and Western) also prohibited one or more forms of racial intermarriage. Reuter points out that in the colonial period, the laws were largely ineffective because although they prevented intermarriage, they could not check miscegenation. He also observed that the lack of legislation forbidding racial intermarriage should not be taken as evidence that such unions are approved or even that there is a general popular indifference to them. The absence of such legislation is rather an expression of the fact that Negroes and Orientals are such a negligible part of the population of several states and intermarriages are so few that the question can be ignored. Moreover, the absence of such legislation is a source of some pride that is luxuriously pleasing. Illinois, Ohio, and New York were the only states with a high proportion of colored people which did not have intermarriage laws. One of these, Ohio, as well as Maine, Massachusetts, and Michigan, once had statutes prohibiting racial intermarriage, but they were later repealed.

A basic conflict in American norms regarding black-white marriage has existed for a long time. In 1927 and 1928 Senator Cole Blease and Representative Allard H. Gasque of South Carolina collaborated with Senator Thaddeus H. Caraway of Arkansas in an unsuccessful attempt to have a law prohibiting black-white marriage passed for the District of Columbia. During 1927 the Ku Klux Klan and others were active in introducing racial intermarriage bills in the legislatures of Connecticut, Maine, Massachusetts, Michigan, New Jersey, and Rhode Island. The bills all died in committee because of the strong opposition of liberal representatives.

After the adoption of the Fourteenth Amendment (proclaimed July 28, 1868) to the Constitution of the United States, the question immediately arose whether or not state laws, prohibiting intermarriage, deny to colored people the equality guaranteed them by the amendment. Many cases testing the constitutionality of these laws were decided in state courts. Invariably, they were held valid.[14]

Antimiscegenation laws were intended to sustain the nineteenth-century social order consistent with the natural-family cultural model, which posits a set of "natural functions in the nuclear family as necessary to uphold the general values and norms of the society." In order to enforce conformity to these norms, the state had to curb impetuous and capricious behavior of family members, who might marry nonconformists or otherwise socially or biologically "undesirable" persons. The state, along with the church, therefore imposed various impediments to a marriage which might endanger the future of society.[15]

Edward B. Reuter states, however, that laws prohibiting racial intermarriage were only as effective as the mores of which they were a formal expression. He believes that the legislation itself probably had no effect at all upon the rate of racial intermixture.[16] In a similar vein, Cloyte M. Larsson recognizes that the history of miscegenation in America teaches that people can be legally separated by walls, but that history also teaches that no walls can be built high enough.[17]

North or South, back door or front door, miscegenation continued. After Appomattox, an increasingly large number of persons used the front door. When the black Republicans came to power, many Southern states changed their legal codes. Mississippi and Louisiana dropped their laws against intermarriage in 1870; Arkansas in 1874; and South Carolina in 1872. However, after the brief period of Black Reconstruction, whites returned to power and again immediately reenacted laws against racial intermarriage.[18]

The Case for and against Racial Endogamy

Richard H. Klemer observes that to many of those who are concerned with civil rights of minority groups, traditional American endogamy—i.e., the custom of requiring individuals to marry within their own racial, religious, and social groups, and so on—has often appeared as a kind of de facto nuptial segregation based on laws as outmoded as the poll tax. The fact that endogamy is prescribed and promoted by conservative moralists and religionists (throughout the country) often damns endogamy by association, regardless of what actual merits it might have. Some object to the traditional pattern of urging people to make conventional, conforming, stable marriages by selecting their partners within their own race, nationality, religion, and social class on the ground that any resulting marital adjustment does not really produce happiness. At best, the argument goes, this endogamy reinforces the antiindividualistic, antipersonal freedom bias of the American middle class, which, although it results in accommodation to the status quo, does not lead to the achievement of positive goals in marriage.

One of the major arguments used against endogamy is the fact that there is a vast and increasing number of people who are happily married to a partner of a different religion, nationality, social status, education, or race. In a society oriented to accepting success as reason enough for overturning tradition and change as a value, this is a powerful argument indeed.[19]

Despite the arguments, pro or con, there still exists in the United States a conflict in norms regarding the right of an individual to select his own marriage partner irrespective of race. A large proportion of American society is intolerant of interracial marriage. In almost every other large and racially mixed society in the modern world such marriages are accepted, both legally and socially. With the exception of the Republic of South Africa, Rhodesia, and possibly Great Britain, no other nation has ever been as determinedly race conscious as the United States.[20]

Based on historical and biological evidence, the idea of a pure race is totally inaccurate. As there is no evidence to support a pure race, neither is there evidence to support the idea that racial mixtures result in biologically inferior offspring. Despite all the evidence disproving superiorities or inferiorities of certain racial groups, many people support this superior-inferior idea via their attitudes, values, and behavior. It is this factor of social definition—the attitudes, values, and resulting behavior—that makes interracial marriage significant. What is dubbed *mixed marriage* or *intermarriage* depends on what differences "make a difference" in the social definition.[21] In the words of Sophia F. McDowell:

> If a Methodist marries a Baptist, a person whose father is a lawyer marries someone whose father is a doctor, or a blue-eyed individual marries a brown-eyed one, we do not speak of "intermarriage," because we do not regard these denominations, occupations, or pigmentations as significantly different from each other. . . . The biological differences between blacks and whites have come to be regarded as terribly important, indeed, although there is no evidence of innate racial distinctions that could be relevant to marriage except those which have been created historically and institutionally.[22]

Nothing would infuriate the average white American male more than his daughter marrying a black. No other mixture touches off such widespread condemnation as race mixing. And no combination of races in the United States epitomizes miscegenation as dramatically as black-white marriages. The problems of any other race mixture are mild by comparison.[23] One of Gunnar Myrdal's[24] theories in his study of the American Negro is the "rank order of discrimination." He maintains that the primary and essential concern of the white man, in his relations with the Negro, is to prevent amalgamation. The closer the relationships come to threatening the antiamalgamation doctrine, the greater are the limitations and restrictions.

Further indication of the significance which groups attach to intermarriage comes from the famous Bogardus[25] social distance test. This scale attempts to measure the reaction of native born Americans to various racial and ethnic groups. Emory S. Bogardus asked 1,725 persons, mostly of North European descent, to indicate to what relationship they were willing to admit the members of various other groups. It was observed that intermarriage is the relationship to which all outgroups are most reluctantly admitted. However, on the other hand, Brewton Berry[26] notes that there is no group, all of whose members are unwilling to have sex relations with individuals in the out-group—a fact amply proved by the hybrid populations which have arisen wherever contacts have occurred. Opposition to intermarriage, of course, may come from either or both of the groups involved; and some groups have developed much more effective techniques than others for enforcing endogamy. At the same time, the mere frequency of out-marriage is not alone proof of assimilation.

INTERMARRIAGE AND MATE SELECTION: A POINT OF VIEW

One of the problems in studying black-white marriages in the United States was observed by Robert K. Merton over thirty years ago. He pointed to the lack of a broad theoretical framework to give scientific unity to the empirical fragments of this phenomenon. Thus, Merton developed such a conceptual model with caste, class, and sex composition.

He sees rates and patterns of intermarriage as being related to cultural orientations, standardized distributions of income and symbols of status; and asserts that the conflicts and accommodations of mates from socially disparate groups are partly understandable in terms of this environing structure.[27] He recognizes however, that his "classification and interpretation are highly provisional and rudimentary: the one needing to be further tested for convenience, the other requiring a larger body of systematically collated data than was yet at hand."[28] While this model served to stimulate research, the findings did not always support Merton's hypotheses (see Chapter 5). Even in recent times, nevertheless, there has been no development of an integrated theory of interracial marriage.

I attempt to modify this current state of "theory," first by briefly-exploring Merton's reasons as to why endogamous rules are so firmly entrenched in all societies; and secondly, by integrating his ideas of rules of endogamy with the notion of "restricted and generalized patterns of exchange" (alliance and descent theories), and the concepts of "orderly replacement vs. permanent availability." Hopefully, these "frames of reference" will generate some additional insight into the dynamics of black-white marriages in this country. An explanation of this analytical scheme is provided in the following section.

Exogamous and Endogamous Rules

The most universal of all norms regarding marriage, the incest taboo, is exogamous. Exogamy rules that members of a society marry outside their kin group. Thus all marriages are exogamous in that they are forbidden between members of the same nuclear family unit. The terms *homogamy* and *endogamy* are generally employed to describe mate selection among those who share similar characteristics. Homogamy denotes something about the likeness or similarity of married couples, whereas endogamy refers to in-group marriages of almost any kind.[29]

Endogamy is a device which serves to maintain social prerogatives and immunities within a social group. It helps prevent the diffusion of power, authority, and preferred status to persons who are not affiliated with a dominant group. It serves further to accentuate and symbolize the "reality" of the group by setting it off against other discriminable social units. Endogamy serves as an isolation and exclusion device, with the function of increasing group solidarity and supporting the social structure by helping to fix social distances which obtain between groups. All this is not meant to imply that endogamy was deliberately instituted for these purposes; this is a description in functional, not necessarily purposive, terms.[30] Homogamy and endogamy are crucial factors in the continuity of the American family system (as well as other social institutions). Homogamy functions to maintain the status quo and conserve traditional values and beliefs.[31]

Bernard Barber claims that in an attempt to perpetuate the status quo, "all societies tend to disapprove not only of all marriage between people from different social classes but also of all social relations between them that could lead to marriage."[32] Kingsley Davis maintains that "a cardinal principle of every stratified society is that the majority of those marrying shall marry equals"; endogamy, or at least preferential in-marriage, is the rule of class, caste, or *stande*. The reason, he claims, is that marriage implies equality. "If some persons are untouchable, they must also be unmarriageable, unusable in the kitchen. For example, a wife reared in a social stratum widely different from her husband's is apt to inculcate ideas and behavior incompatible with the position the children will inherit from their father, thus creating a hiatus between their status and their role."[33]

Restricted and Generalized Exchange

A closer examination of kin relationships provides additional insight into the functional nature of endogamous norms. In the study of kinship organization, researchers have made extensive use of two theoretical frameworks—the "alliance" and "descent" approaches. Alliance theory assumes that kinship structures derive their form from the regulation of marital exchange. Descent theory is concerned with rules or devices that preserve the continuity of the lineage. These theoretical viewpoints can be regarded as complementary rather than conflicting.[34]

Claude Lévi-Strauss' *Elementary Kinship Structures* (1969) focuses attention on kinship systems as methods of organizing marriage relations between groups. He argues that kinship groups were simply units in a system of "alliances" made or "expressed" by marriage.[35] Bernard Farber notes that for Lévi-Strauss, in marital transactions, people represent a commodity essentially like all other goods (such as cattle, land, or tools). Therefore, members of kin groups themselves are included in the category of property.[36] Moreover, some of the group's most important assets are its wives and daughters.[37] In a summarization of Lévi-Strauss' views of marital exchange, Robin Fox reports that in relation to the descent approach, kinship systems are seen as mechanisms for the formation and recruitment of property owning, residential, and political groups, etc. This perspective might be referred to as the "genetic" (restricted exchange) model for the integration of groups on the basis of their real or assumed common ancestry. Thus, clanship and segmentary lineage organization are seen as devices to this end.[38]

Elementary systems of exchange are concerned with "exchange and alliance." Whatever the units involved—families, bands, lineages, clans, moieties, tribes—they enter into relations of exchange with each other and form alliances. Once an alliance has been formed, it is perpetuated—i.e., once two groups have exchanged women, they continue to do so. This has the effect of laying down not only the category of persons whom one may *not* marry (same clan or family, parallel cousins etc.) but also that into which one *must* marry.

The systems differ in the ways in which they organize this positive marriage rule. This implies two alternatives: as far as any unit is concerned, its "wife givers" are either the same as its "wife takers," or they are different. If they are the same, then this involves the principle of "straight swaps"; if they are different, then women are not being directly exchanged but instead circulated around the system.

Lévi-Strauss has characterized the first kind of system as "restricted exchange" and the second as "generalized exchange." Exchange is "restricted" where it has to include two groups who exchange directly. Such a system can only grow by splitting into four, eight, sixteen etc. groups and by continuing to exchange directly. This might suit small populations with a small number of groups, but it is difficult to run it with large and complex societies. The "generalized" method on the other hand, can expand indefinitely. Any number of groups and any number of cycles can be involved.[39]

Generally, property may be regarded as something which may be withheld or prohibited from exchange (for example, entailed estate cannot be sold). According to Lévi-Strauss, property then is nonreciprocity. Kin groups can vary in the amount and value of property they possess. Social position of a kin group therefore depends upon the extent of surplus value of assets over what is required for exchange. Viewed from this perspective, social structure is molded by regulations which govern the accumulation, inheritance, distribution, and transmission of kin-group property by inhibiting exchange and dissipation of this property.

From the viewpoint of perpetuation of kin-group property, marital exchange is a necessary evil unless it can be applied in such a way as: (1) to perpetuate this property by requiring persons with preexisting consanguineous ties to marry one another (as in direct exchange of siblings) or to arrange marriages of relatives (as in indirect exchange); or (2) to simultaneously enhance the assets of both kin groups involved in the marriage.

In the case of "complex structures," where greater latitude exists in marital selection, there is an ambivalence between pressures for exchange and those for accumulation and perpetuation of kin-group property. The resolution of the conflict between these opposing forces depends upon the value of kinship property. In highly industrial societies, kin groups with valuable property become highly selective in establishing close ties with other kin groups through marriage. Oftentimes, situations exist in which a kin group does not want to establish a cooperative relationship with another group. In American society, religious and racial intermarriage is often discouraged on this basis.[40]

In a similar manner, David M. Heer also observes that restriction on racial intermarriage may be closely linked to economic discrimination. In reference to familial inheritance, on a per capita basis whites hold a far higher share of the nation's wealth than do blacks. The formal and informal prohibitions on intermarriage serve to perpetuate this pattern of inequality since they make it unlikely that blacks will inherit wealth from whites. Second, blacks are by and large excluded from those jobs to which entrance is strongly determined by pull and connections. Third, the lack of close relatives among whites prevents many blacks from having an easy familiarity of the social world of whites and hence makes them reluctant to apply for jobs demanding such familiarity, even when their technical qualifications are completely satisfactory. A relaxation of the norms militating against miscegenation, then, might have a significant and crucial effect on the socioeconomic position of black Americans.[41]

Other societies often provide striking implications of interclass/caste marriage patterns. For example, in contemporary

Great Britain, patterns of marital mobility are changing. The English aristocracy, while being largely endogamous, has nevertheless "married down" a good deal. Younger sons have often married heiresses to boost the family fortunes. Evidence from novels suggests that with the expansion of higher education, there is a flow up the ladder of boys from artisan homes who marry middle-class girls as part of their pattern of social mobility. Regarding the strains and hostilities involved in such marriages, in the future, the relative endogamy of racial groups will provide yet another complication. While it is hard to compare Western society with primitive societies which are composed of extended kin groups as the basic unit, one can easily look at it as a variant on the alliance theme and ask how women (and men for that matter) are distributed around the system through marriage, and what the directions and intensities of these flows are. Fox notes that if we are looking for the channels along which alliances flow, then we move into this wider sociological perspective which may give us new insights into the dynamics of our own society.[42]

Orderly Replacement vs. Permanent Availability

To add a corollary to the alliance approach, Farber suggests a theory that not only explains the continuity of familial values and norms but also the changing values and norms in contemporary kinship and family systems. The family, he says, should be regarded in terms of a lineage system or "orderly replacement" and the availability of individuals for marriage—"permanent availability." If orderly replacement is to occur, each family of orientation must provide for the continuance of its values and norms relating to patterns of family life and the socialization of children. Each family then serves to transmit cultural patterns.[43]

It is Farber's assumption that every society has both of the above tendencies in varying proportions; however, given certain conditions, one may predominate over the other. For example, unilineal kinship and/or closed systems with norms related to preferential and prescribed marriages are structurally best able to maintain orderly replacement of family culture. On the other hand, in bilateral kinship and/or open systems, lineage considerations in mate selection are at a minimum and kinship control over marriages dissipates. As a result, individuals become available for marriage with anyone at any time during their adulthood. Thus, in bilateral systems, a greater tendency probably exists for people to marry outside their particular cultural system.

There is however, a continuing conflict in contemporary urban, industrial societies between these two aspects (orderly replacement vs. permanent availability) of the family because in reality (a) each nuclear family is to some extent a closed system isolated from other families; and (b) some restrictions do exist with regard to availability as a mate even in bilateral systems. Yet, the conflict tends to be resolved in favor of permanent availability.

An important point in this connection is that recognized change is occurring in the significance of certain traditional categories. Social-class lines are becoming blurred; ethnic groups are losing their specific identity as their members become more diffused among the various socioeconomic statuses and institutions of the society. As the various segments of the populations lose their visibility, barriers to intermarriage are dissolved. In spite of the tendency for old categories to persist, other categories of mate selection will likely increase in relative importance. Other aspects of homogamy are not so much concerned with traditional categories of social life (like race, religion, social class, and ethnic groups) as with community background, personal interest, personality characteristics, and physical characteristics of the couple. As homogamy based upon traditional categories declines, homogamy based on personal characteristics can be expected to become the primary factor in mate selection.[44] It is suggested that the conceptual frameworks described above—i.e., restricted and generalized models of exchange (alliance and descent) and orderly replacement vs. permanent availability guide this investigation.

2

Incidence and Nature of Black-White Marriages

WHILE STATES DO collect marriage data, some gather no information on the race of the marriage applicants. Among those which do, few actually publish statistics on intermarriage; and the statistics which are available are not always reliable. National statistics are also incomplete. The United States Census publishes reports on the marital status of the population which include some data on mixed marriages. These data however, are estimates, based on a 5 percent sample, which provide information on intermarriage for the entire country and for several regions, but not for the separate states. The use of population samples magnifies this problem because sample selection tends to depend on availability rather than a full knowledge of the universe. Generally, samples have been quite small.[1] Although the National Center for Health Statistics reports on marriage occurrences which include certain racial data for selected states and areas, black-white intermarriage figures are not reported.[2]

It is exceedingly difficult to determine the frequency of black-white marriage. What compounds the problem even more is classifying an individual into a given racial group. If a black passes for white and marries a white, is this an intermarriage or an endogamous marriage? If a person is one-eighth or one-sixteenth black (as black is defined on the law books of various states), would it not be an intermarriage irrespective of which race one marries? Even if a categorization could be agreed upon and precisely determined, one could argue that social sanctions against such marriages are so severe in most parts of the United States that the reported number of such marriages would be less than the actual number. Due to the questionable validity of the reported numbers of interracial marriages, extreme caution should be taken in the interpretation of any data.[3] Keeping in mind the limitations of available data, I examine the demographic and legal trends of black-white marriages in the United States in this chapter. Second, I explore the dynamics of the social context of these unions from around 1897 up to about 1964.

Demographic Trends

The earliest series of statistical data on black-white marriages appear to be those published by Frederick L. Hoffman, W. E. B. Dubois, Ray S. Baker, Richard R. Wright, A. H. Stone, Gilbert T. Stephenson, Julius Drachsler, J. V. DePorte, and Louis Wirth and Herbert Goldhamer.[4] The national frequency of racial intermarriage today is not known. It has been conservatively estimated at no more than about 2,000 per year, or about one in every 1,200 marriages. Figures are available for New York State and Boston for the early years of this century and for upstate New York from 1916 to 1964, and for California, Hawaii, Michigan, and Nebraska during the 1950s and 1960s. For the period 1916 through 1937, black-white marriages in New York State exclusive of New York City varied from 1.7 to 4.8 percent of all marriages involving blacks. The equivalent percentages for whites would be even lower. In Boston, the highest period of racial intermarriage appears to have been 1850-1900. In the 1900-1904 period and the 1914-1918 period, the racial intermarriage rate declined from 14 to 5 per 100 marriages involving blacks. Since that time, the rate of intermarriage in Boston has averaged 3.9 per 100 black marriages and 0.12 per 100 white marriages, with a slight but perceptible decline up until the Second World War. The decline in intermarriages in Boston after the turn of the century was almost entirely due to a decline in marriages involving black grooms and white brides. Figures for Boston after 1938 are unavailable.[5] Table 2-1 provides a statistical summary of these trends from 1874-1937.

Thomas P. Monahan also examined intermarriage statistics in upstate New York from 1916 to 1964. From 1916 to 1921 the percent of nonwhite marriages and black marriages that were mixed rose to a high point in 1921, when 7.6 percent of the nonwhite and 6.2 percent of black marriages were mixed. Thereafter there was a gradual decline until 1950 when 2.7 percent of all nonwhite and 1.5 percent of black marriages were mixed. An upward trend reasserted itself in 1951 with a dramatic rise from 1958 to 1964. The percentage for all nonwhite marriages over that time period went from 4 in 1958 to 5, 6.4, 6, 6.5, 7.2, and 8.6. For blacks it went from 2.1 in 1958 to 2.5, 3.4, 3.5, 5, 4.5, and 5.6. One could expect a continued increase if racial barriers are leveled and intermingling occurs.[6]

John H. Burma, in a study of interracial marriages in Los Angeles County from 1948 to 1959, found that such marriages were increasing at a significant rate. Some 3,200 were recorded, with black-white and Filipino-white marriages the most common. California's law against intermarriage was declared unconstitutional by the Supreme Court of that state. At the end of the eleven-year period, the rates were about triple of those at the beginning of the period.[7]

A recent analysis of the statistics for the 1950s and 1960s has also been made by Heer. In only three states was there any officially published record of such intermarriages: Hawaii (1956-64), Michigan (1953-63), and Nebraska (1961-64). For selected years (1955, 1957, 1958, and 1959), the state of California made public a cross-tabulation of marriages by race of

Table 2-1

Summary of Earlier Studies of the Number of Black-White Intermarriages: 1874–1937

Researcher	Area	Period	Number of Intermarriages	Average per Year
Hoffman	Michigan	1874–1893	111	5.5
Hoffman	Connecticut	1883–1893	65	5.9
Hoffman	Rhode Island	1883–1893	58	5.3
Hoffman	Boston	1855–1887	600	18.2
Dubois[a]	Philadelphia	1896–1897	33	.....
Baker[b]	Boston	1899–1905	171	.....
Wright	Philadelphia	1900	6	.....
Stone	Boston	1900–1904	143	28.6
Stephenson	Boston	1900–1907	222	27.7
Wright	Philadelphia	1901–1904	21	5.2
Drachsler	New York City	1908–1912	52	10.4
Wirth and Goldhamer	Boston	1914–1938	276	5.4
DePorte	New York State	1919–1929	347	31.5
Wirth and Goldhamer[c]	New York State	1916–1937	569	.....

Sources: Louis Wirth and Herbert Goldhamer, "The Hybrid and the Problem of Miscegenation," in Otto Kline-berg, ed., *Characteristics of the American Negro* (New York: Harper and Row, 1944), p. 277.
[a]W. E. B. Dubois, *The Philadelphia Negro: A Social Study* (New York: Schocken, 1967), pp. 358–367. These find-ings are based on couples living in Philadelphia's Seventh Ward only.
[b]Edward B. Reuter, *The Mulatto in the United States* (Boston: Gorham Press, 1918), p. 135.
[c]Exclusive of New York City.

bride and groom. However, in 1969, new legislation prohibited this practice. In all four states (for the period studied) the trend in recent years has been for a rise both in the proportion of white men marrying black women and of black men marrying white women.[8] A closer look at the state of Hawaii indicates how extensive interracial marriage could become under conditions of freedom of the races. Monahan, utilizing the published statistics for Hawaii, charted the distribution of interracial marriage for a seven-year period, 1956 to 1962. Thirty-seven percent of all marriages were intermarriages. These marriages included Black, Korean, Puerto Rican, Japanese, Filipino, Chinese, Hawaiian, and Caucasian.[9]

Moreover, Larsson observes that within recent years, there has been a rather dramatic rise in the number of interracial marriages among artists, entertainers, bohemians, intellectuals, and the personnel of interracial social agencies. Marriage clerks, social workers, and counselors interviewed by *Jet* in a recent survey said the trend is also on the upswing among ordinary people and is likely to continue with increasing integration. She also notes that an increasing number of white men are marrying black women.[10]

Thus, by piecing together the earlier and later data, though they are from different locations, it may be tentatively concluded that the rate of black-white intermarriage has been curvilinear, declining from the late 1900s to about 1940, and rising gradually since that time.[11]

Changes in the Social Climate

Despite the strong opposition in this country there has been an increase in interracial relationships recently. Henry A. Bowman observes that this increase seems to be due to factors such as the Second World War—during which many American servicemen married Oriental women, urbanization, the influx of foreign students and other visitors, the extension of American business and political interests throughout the world, and the increased intermingling of peoples.[12] To these factors may be added others. For example, the 1954 Supreme Court's decision (*Brown* vs. *Board of Education*), the rising self-consciousness of black people, and the enactment of certain laws, particularly the Civil Rights Acts of 1964 and 1965, have repudiated and dismantled the legal structure of segregation and separation.[13] Still another factor is the cause-and-effect relationship between social change and acceptance of it. In turn, growing acceptance of it facilitates increased frequency. To some degree a social phenomenon is the cause of its own proliferation. The more racial intermarriage occurs, the more it is likely to occur and be accepted in the general population.[14]

In a similar vein, Heer's study of interracial marriages emphasizes status difference between blacks and whites. In this connection, he suggests that the increase in black-white marriages is caused by several other factors. There has been a rise in status for many black families, and increased education and income mean that there are more potential white partners at comparable status levels. Also, there has been a decrease in residential and educational segregation in many of the census areas studied. This closer proximity probably involves more frequent opportunities for social contact, dating, and eventual marriage. More tolerant and liberal attitudes toward blacks in general may also be a factor. However, Heer does not think that the combination of these factors will provide any dramatic increase in the rate of black-white marriages in the next 100 years.[15]

Liberalized admissions policies at American universities and colleges have also mixed more black and white students, and it is now commonplace to see interracial couples strolling in college towns. The Peace Corps and Vista have been indirectly responsible for further interracial dating and intermarriage. Social activism has also established a solid common ground for white and nonwhite youths.[16]

Changes in Antimiscegenation Laws

Also contributing to the rising rate of mixed marriages are the recent changes in antimiscegenation or intermarriage laws in the United States. As recently as 1960, twenty-nine states, mostly Southern and Western, still had such laws. In 1964, it was nineteen states; in 1966, seventeen; and in 1967 it was sixteen.[17] The United States Supreme Court in its historic decision in June 1967 struck down as unconstitutional a 1924 Virginia law forbidding marriage between members of different races. According to the court, a law of this type violates rights guaranteed to all persons under the Fourteenth Amendment to the Constitution.

The case involved two native-born Virginians, Richard Loving, a white man, and Mildred, his wife, who was part black and part American Indian. In June 1958, they were married in the District of Columbia. Shortly after their marriage, the Lovings returned to Virginia and established their marital abode in Caroline County. At the October term, 1958, of the Circuit Court of Caroline County, a grand jury issued an indictment charging the Lovings with violating Virginia's ban on interracial marriages. On January 6, 1959, the Lovings pleaded guilty to the charge and were sentenced to one year in jail; however, the trial judge suspended the sentence for a period of twenty-five years on the condition that the Lovings leave the state and not return to Virginia together for twenty-five years. He stated in an opinion that:

> Almighty God created the races white, black, yellow, malay and red, and he placed them on separate continents. And but for the interference with his arrangement there would be no cause for such marriages. The fact that he separated the races shows that he did not intend for the races to mix.

After their convictions, the Lovings took up residence in the District of Columbia. On November 6, 1963, they filed a motion in the state trial court to vacate the judgment and set aside the sentence on the ground that the statutes which they had violated were repugnant to the Fourteenth Amendment.

The statutes under which the Lovings were convicted and sentenced are part of a comprehensive statutory scheme aimed at prohibiting and punishing interracial marriages. The Lovings were convicted of violating a Virginia Code:

> *Leaving the State to Evade Law.*—If any white person shall go out of this State, for the purpose of being married, and with the intention of returning and be married out of it, and afterwards return to and reside in it, cohabiting as man and wife, they shall be punished; and the marriage shall be governed by the same law as if it had been solemnized in this State.

The penalty for miscegenation, provides:

> *Punishment for Marriage.*—If any white person intermarry with a colored person, or any colored person intermarry with a white person, he shall be guilty of a felony and shall be punished by confinement in the penitentiary for not less than one nor more than five years.

After a series of court battles, the Lovings' case was finally decided upon by the Supreme Court of the United States. Mr. Chief Justice Warren delivered the opinion of the Court:

> This case presents a constitutional question never addressed by this Court: whether a statutory scheme adopted by the State of Virginia to prevent marriages between persons solely on the basis of racial classifications violates the Equal Protection and Due Process Clauses of the Fourteenth Amendment. For reasons which seem to us to reflect the central meaning of these constitutional commands, we conclude that these statutes cannot stand consistently with the Fourteenth Amendment.[18]

Numerous states, however, still have laws on their books which prohibit marriages between persons of different races. The most frequently prohibited type of marriage relationship is between blacks and whites. Even as we entered the 1970s, at least twelve states prohibited marriage between whites and Orientals and at least six states prohibited marriage between whites and American Indians.[19]

The United States Supreme Court recognizes the freedom to marry as one of the "vital personal rights" or "basic civil rights of man" which is essential to the orderly pursuit of happiness by free men.[20] The act of marriage itself then has replaced the particular form of marriage and family life as a "natural" phenomenon. It follows that what is done or how things are done in any particular family are matters of private and not public or legal concern. This situation opens the way for a wide differentiation of styles of family life in the society.[21] However, despite the lack of legal support for bans on interracial marriage, the customs and norms of the white majority, and to some extent the black minority, make interracial marriage a "rare and deviant" sort of behavior.

THE SOCIAL CONTEXT OF BLACK-WHITE MARRIAGES: 1897-1964

As mentioned earlier, research on black-white marriages is limited and sparse. The scarcity of data is due in some measure to the lack of interest or indifference of many social scientists. Moreover, careful research in this area is as difficult as it is expensive, and the limited amount of study which has been done reflects in part the dearth of research grants which in turn indicates the low priority given this type research. There is also some concern that black-white marriages are strictly private affairs, and are therefore not a province for sociological inquiry.[22]

It is true that no large-scale and systematic studies have been conducted in this area. Therefore, few definitive generalizations can be made regarding the interactional patterns of black-white families in the United States. However, some few inquiring individuals, using small samples, have studied this complex and traditionally tabooed subject. A discussion of some of their findings follows. The central focus is on: (1) frequency and combination of the intermarried, (2) social "types" who marry across racial lines, (3) the stability of these unions, (4) adjustment problems of the children, (5) relations with the larger community, and (6) family strategies developed to deal with various issues.

Frequency and Combination

The large majority of the mixed marriages in the early part of this century consisted of Negro or mulatto men and white women. In 158 of the 171 cases reported by Baker, the groom was Negro and the bride white. In thirteen cases the groom was white. Of the fifty-eight mixed marriages in Rhode Island, fifty-one involved white females and seven, white males. Of the 111 cases in Michigan, ninety-three included white women, and eighteen white men. In this connection, of the eighteen white men married to Negroes, six married black females, and twelve mulatto females. Of the ninety-three whites married to Negroes, forty-seven were married to black males and forty-six to mulatto males.

Stone reports that of the fifty-two mixed marriages in thirty-seven towns and cities of the state of Massachusetts in 1900, forty-three were between white women and Negro men. During the five years from 1900 to 1904, there were 143 marriages between Negroes and whites in the city of Boston. Of these mixed marriages, 133 were cases consisting of white women and black men, while only ten white men were married to black women. Stone also suggests that the same marital combinations existed in Chicago, Philadelphia, and New York.[23]

As part of a larger study of Negro life in Philadelphia in 1897, Dubois studied thirty-three cases of black-white marriages in the Seventh Ward. There were other couples in this area, and probably a similar proportion in many other wards. Of these thirty-three couples, only four consisted of white males-black females.[24]

On the basis of 325 cases of intermarriage reported to Ray E. Baber by his students in his Marriage and the Family course at New York University, there were twenty-five cases of black-white marriages—of which eighteen consisted of black males-white females. As for this sample, black men married white women four times as frequently as white men married black women.[25]

Wirth and Goldhamer reported some of their findings based upon data taken from the original marriage licenses issued by the Registry Department of the City of Boston for the period 1914-1938. The most striking feature of these data was the extremely high rate of Negro-white intermarriages for Boston in the years immediately after 1900—from 5.2 percent in 1914 to 3.7 percent in 1938. During the period 1914-1938, there were 276 black-white marriages in Boston (227 black male-white female, and forty-nine white male-black female combinations). Three-hundred and ninety out of every 10,000 blacks who married in Boston during the years 1914-1918 married white persons. Only thirteen out of every 10,000 white persons marrying there, married a black. Outmarriage between blacks and whites during this period was thirty times greater among blacks than among whites.[26]

Social Characteristics of the Intermarried

These mixed marriages as a rule are of the lower classes of whites. The women in most of the unions are recent immigrants and often, no doubt, contract the alliances without realizing the social consequences. P. A. Bruce observes that:

> The few white women who have given birth to mulattoes have always been regarded as monsters; and without exception, they have belonged to the most impoverished and degraded caste of whites, by whom they are scrupulously avoided as creatures who have sunk to the level of the beasts of the field.

Of the thirty-seven cases of mixed couples studied by Hoffman, twenty-nine consisted of white women living with Negro men; and eight were of white men living with black women. Of the eight white men, four were legally married and four were not. Three of them were criminals or criminal suspects. The others were considered outcasts: one was a saloon keeper, one had deserted a white wife and family, and two others were of good families but were themselves of bad reputations. Of the twenty-nine white women, nineteen were lawfully married to their Negro husbands, while ten were living in open concubinage. Five of these latter were foreign born. Eight of the number were prostitutes, one was insane, and one was the daughter of respectable parents. Of the nineteen who were lawfully married, four were prostitutes, two were guilty of bigamy, four were either divorced or had deserted husbands, five were apparently of respectable parentage and contented with their husbands. Of the four others, Hoffman was able to obtain no information.

Of the twenty-nine Negro men, one was an industrious barber of good character, five were of fair repute, nine were idlers, loafers, or drunkards, and eleven were proved criminal. The character of the remaining three was not determined.

Hoffman concludes by saying:

> Comment on these cases is hardly necessary. They tend to prove that as a rule neither good white men nor good white women marry colored persons, and that good colored men and women do not marry white persons. The number of cases is so small, however, that a definite conclusion as to the character of persons intermarrying is hardly warranted. However, it would seem that if such marriages were a success, even to a limited extent, some evidence would be found in a collection of 36 cases. It is my opinion, based on personal observation in cities of the South, that individuals of both races who intermarry or live in concubinage are vastly inferior to the average types of the whites and colored races in the United States; also that the class of white men who have intercourse with colored women are, as a rule, of an inferior type.

These mixed marriages are frequently marriages of mulattoes, usually light-colored mulattoes, with the poorer and lower class of white women. Not infrequently, it would seem the unions take place without the girl realizing that she is marrying a Negro. Cases where such facts are made the grounds for divorce proceedings, appear from time to time in the daily press.[27]

Dubois reports in his Philadelphia study that the birth places of the white husbands were: Pennsylvania, Georgia,

Cuba, and one unknown; of the black wives: Maryland, Georgia, Virginia, and one unknown. Eight of the black husbands were born in the North, and nineteen in the South. Two of the husbands' birth places were unknown. The median age of this group upon contracting this marriage tended to be higher than that of the general population.[28] Of the seven white grooms in Baber's study, only two were born in the United States. Of the eighteen white brides, ten were born in America.

According to Dubois, the social grade (social status) of thirty-two of the thirty-three mixed families was thought to be as follows: *First grade*, four families; they lived well and were comfortable; the wife did not work. *Second grade*, there were fifteen families; ordinary working-class families, in which the wife in some cases, helped as breadwinner. None in this group were poverty stricken; many were young couples with decency and respectability. *Third grade*, six families who were poor but not immoral; some were lazy, some unfortunate. *Fourth grade*, seven families; many of these were cases of permanent cohabitation in which the women, for the most part, were or had been prostitutes. They lived in the slums. None of them had children or at least was living with them. There was a total of thirty-one children and twenty other relatives in these families; twenty-seven of the children were born of white mothers and four of black mothers.

Dubois' findings did not support the hypothesis that only low status blacks and white intermarry. He noted that among the lowest classes, there was a large number of temporary unions and much cohabitation. Marriage took place most frequently in the laboring classes, and especially among servants where there was the most contact between the races. Among the highest class of blacks and whites, such marriages seldom occurred. However, one notable case occurred in Philadelphia in 1897.[30]

A study of employed Negro males in Boston demonstrated that the racially intermarried Negro grooms occupied superior occupational positions as compared with all gainfully employed Negro males. Slightly over 60 percent of the latter were unskilled workers as compared with slightly over 40 percent of the Negro grooms contracting mixed marriages. White grooms, on the other hand, exhibited a reverse tendency. Whereas only 19 percent of the gainfully employed white males in Boston were in unskilled occupations slightly over 40 percent of the white grooms of racial intermarriage were in this class. Among the gainfully employed white females in Boston, 15.7 percent were unskilled workers, whereas 63.6 percent of the white brides of racial intermarriage fell in this occupational group. The Negro brides also showed an overrepresentation of unskilled workers.

Wirth and Goldhamer also observed that the light-skinned black male sought out a white wife to enhance his esteem. Foreign-born white males married black women "to a greater extent than their representation in the general population" and there was an overrepresentation of native-born white females in black-white marriages. For this group, the median age for black grooms was 29.1, for white grooms 31.6, and 26.0 and 23.9 for black and white brides respectively. The median age for all black spouses was 28.6, and 25.2 for white and 27.4 for the entire group.[31]

Of the black-white couples studied in Chicago, St. Clair Drake and Horace Cayton found that among whites, racial intermarriage seemed to have disproportionately involved the widowed or divorced, older persons, urban people, native-born white women and foreign-born men, and white women of a low social status. The blacks were intellectuals, bohemians, members of cults, and lower-class individuals without race pride.[32]

Studies made by Joseph Golden in Philadelphia corroborated the findings of Drake and Cayton. Even though there were no laws forbidding it, intermarriage in Philadelphia was not extensive. The intermarried couples (50) had a median education which amounted to high-school completion. The data did not confirm the prevailing opinion that well-educated black men marry ignorant white women. Of forty-four black men, seventeen had married white women on the same education level, twelve had married educationally downward, while fifteen had married upward. In terms of the occupational matching of the spouses, a tendency was found toward homogamy. On the other hand, less than half of the marriages were religiously homogamous.[33]

While there is some consensus on certain aspects of interracial marriage, contradictions can be found in the literature.[34] At one time it was hypothesized, as indicated by Davis,[35] Wirth and Goldhamer,[36] and E. Franklin Frazier,[37] that such interracial marriages involved a prosperous Negro man and a lower class white woman. A study by Todd H. Pavela[38] of ninety-five Negro-white marriages recorded in Indiana for 1958-59, however, did not support this hypothesis. The occupational distribution of the partners was the same as for Indiana marriages as a whole. There was no indication of a pattern of occupational dominance of one spouse over another, regardless of race. Pavela further points out that it appears that such marriages are now socioeconomically homogamous. Jessie Bernard[39] also concluded after a study of the 1960 census data, that Negro-white marriages tend to be educationally homogamous in about the same proportion as marriages between people of the same race.

Children of Black-White Marriages

Albert I. Gordon asserted that children, more often than their parents, are the victims of intermarriage because of the uncertainty concerning their identity. Intermarried parents find it difficult to provide their children with the security that comes from "knowing *who* I am and *what* I am." He states that children of mixed marriages are faced with problems which tend to produce within them reactions of guilt, insecurity, anxiety, and emotional instability. He further comments that children who would like to identify with both parents find themselves torn between the loyalty they feel they owe each parent. As a consequence of their inability to identify with *both* parents, a feeling of resentment develops against one or both parents.[40]

John Dollard noted that much has been made of the special problems experienced everywhere by lighter-skinned Negroes. Part of the social insecurity of the lighter Negro unquestionably stems from the conflict often represented in his appearance. The nearer he approximates Caucasoid physical features, the more likely it is that he is a result of tabooed sexual contacts. This ambivalent attitude toward physical ancestry showed up repeatedly in the reports of his Negro informants on their genealogies. They were proud of their white ancestors, but related to this pride in the sense of being scorned and rejected.[41]

Baber reported that the children in the black-white families he studied were particularly handicapped; they literally had no "race," frequently being rejected by both groups. Such terms as *half-breed, half-caste, mulatto,* and *Eurasian* usually carried disapproval and sometimes scorn. The chances of intrafamily strife were increased. Frequently within the same family, one child was white and another black.

He cites one case (white male-black female), in which the boy was white and his two sisters dark. They quarreled a great deal—his most effective technique was to call them "nigger," which infuriated the girls and stirred up both parents. In another case (black male-white female), the small black daughter hated her mother for being white, but loved her father because he was black as she was. Her small brother, however, loved his mother, but hated his sister for disliking and striking the mother. Still another mother (white male-black female) was hurt because her daughters avoided introducing her to their friends as their mother, but were eager to introduce their father and show him off.[42]

According to Drake and Cayton, most of the children (in their sample) light-skinned enough to pass usually solved their problem ultimately by doing so. Some left their parents while at young ages; others waited until their education was completed or until their parents died. With no strong family ties, and few roots in the black community, passing was the logical way out of a difficult situation. The majority, however, made a successful adjustment in the black community. It was difficult for these children to make a social adjustment, but they were not invariably unhappy.

    They found that some couples had not informed white relatives of the existence of children for fear they (children) would be rejected. Moreover, it was seldom that the white relatives, even though somewhat tolerant of the intermarriage, welcomed the offspring. In rearing their children, the couples faced a number of problems incomprehensible to those who had married within the conventional patterns.

Relations with the Larger Community

Drake and Cayton also observed that these families often experienced difficulties in obtaining and holding jobs, and in securing a place to live. They were subject to ostracism from the community, friends, and relatives.[43] In a similar vein, Golden notes that prior to marriage, the couples had been forced to conduct a "sub rosa courtship." The wedding ceremony continued the pattern of secrecy, being civil rather than religious. These families had difficulties in finding residential quarters; they usually lived in peripheral areas on the border between white and black communities. Other problems included occupational adjustments, relations with friends, churches, and the community. A sizeable proportion had been previously married. Golden ventures the guess that these families felt so insecure that they refrained from inviting the additional hazard of children. There were not many children. The median age of 28.3 for both spouses at marriage might partially account for this fact.[44]

Charles E. Smith reports in his study of some thirty-nine New York middle-class, black-white couples that both partners often received stares from strangers, interrogation by new friends, and occasional "beatings" by new enemies. Forceful intervention by unofficial strangers was rare, however, compared to the "rather common" experience of these couples being stopped by strange officials on the highways. Policemen could hardly imagine that a black-white couple might be married. The woman was assumed to be either a prostitute or maid; the man either a rapist or chauffeur. To minimize hostile reactions from the community, these couples often hid their relationship from public view. They rarely announced their engagements publicly, rationalizing that "society would do a rather thorough job of 'doing that anyway'."

Smith further notes that external persecution sometimes drew husband and wife closer together. However, outside pressures had at least occasional inside repercussions. The Negro partner tended to be supersensitized by his experiences. The original establishment of relationship usually depended on overtures from the white partner since most blacks were afraid of being rejected if they made any advances. After marriage, the black partner tended to be touchy about racial slurs and insisted on the white partner's need to learn to "understand" Negroes. Alienation from parents was the most difficult emotional problem reported by the white spouses.[45]

Marital Stability

Concerning the stability of these marriages, it has been reported that those who contract a black-white marriage are more likely to become divorced.[46] Dubois reported that available data at the early part of this century were not adequate (including his own) and representative enough to make broad generalizations regarding divorce rates for this group. It was likely, however, that more separations occurred in these marriages than in others. "It is certainly a strain on affections to have to endure not simply the social ostracism of the whites, but of the blacks also."[47]

Baber found that white male-black female marriages were much lower on the happiness scale than those of the black male-white female combination. He suggested that the greater the

color difference, the smaller the chance for happiness. The proportions of widowed persons among Negro and white grooms
and brides in this study were also markedly in excess of those
in the total Negro and white populations of the city for comparable age groups. Moreover, the average age at marriage was
well above that for the general population. Over 30 percent of
the Negro and white brides had been previously married; and
in a few cases (8 percent for the Negro brides, and 1 percent for
the white brides), the interracial marriage represented a third
marriage. The percentage of previously married persons was
almost as high for the Negro grooms as for the Negro and
white brides, but appreciably lower for the white grooms.[48]

Wirth and Goldhamer's data reveal similar patterns. For
example, of the forty-nine white grooms in the group, not a
single one had been divorced. The bulk of the Negro grooms
ranged within the ages of twenty-five to forty-four. The census of 1930 showed the 1.3 percent of Boston male Negroes in
this age group were divorced as compared with 11.5 percent for
the Negro intermarried grooms. Similarly, for the twenty to
forty-four age range (which contained the bulk of the Negro
brides), according to the 1930 census, 2.5 percent of the Negro
females of Boston were divorced, which contrasted with 12.2
percent of the intermarried Negro brides. The white brides'
divorce rate was also practically identical with that of the Negro grooms and brides.[49]

It is not surprising that strong United States norms
against racial intermarriage should be accompanied by beliefs
that such marriages are fraught with special hazard and more
likely to fail than are racially homogamous marriages.[50] However, except for some nonconfirming information on the State
of Hawaii, in recent years, nothing is known statistically to
support this thesis of instability.[51] As William M. Kephart
says, "No divorce statistics are available which would enable
us to generalize about their instability."[52] Moreover, Monahan's analysis of a small set of data (published and unpub-
lished records) on the State of Iowa for 1940-67, indicates the

divorce rate for black-black couples to be about twice as high as that for whites. But black-white marriages are more stable than black-black, and black husbands and white wives have a lower divorce outcome than do white couples.[53]

In this same connection, Golden concluded that the black-white marriages in Philadelphia had a good chance of survival. Pavela comments on the Indiana sample: "These were not impulsive teenage marriages. These couples have a strong emotional attachment, be it rationalization or real." Although external pressures were often great they certainly did not appear to be overwhelming.[54]

Strategies to Deal with Specific Problems

Among the postwar phenomena of the American social scene was a considerable increase in mixed marriages. This was given impetus by black servicemen who brought brides home from abroad in World War II. Immediately after the war, in order to find companionship and face more easily the problems of a mixed marriage, many couples organized clubs whose memberships were restricted to persons who had married across the color line.

The largest of the clubs was the Club Miscegenation organized in Los Angeles. There was also one located in Washington, D.C.—Club Internationale, organized in 1947 by fourteen couples, ten of them black exservicemen. The smallest, Detroit's Club of Tomorrow, had only a half dozen mixed couples, but hoped to attract other members from the 500 interracially married pairs said to live in the area. Some of these clubs were still functioning in the early 1950s. From all indications, this is not true today.

The clubs had a history dating back to 1890, when the Manassah Society was organized in Milwaukee. Spreading to Chicago, it had a membership of 700 after the turn of the century and had become one of the city's elite organizations. A similar group, New York City's Penguin Club, was established in 1936. Its 100 couples were admitted only after careful investigations of character. Couples without children were not accepted, because only parenthood was regarded as positive proof "of the stability of the relationship."

When the members met, they would play cards, attend picnics, hold an occasional educational "do," and discuss their common problems, which were numerous. Talking could only rarely produce a solution for the aggrieved person, but it helped to fight the feeling of isolation. The members admitted that social ostracism led them to form these exclusive organizations.[59]

SUMMARY

A majority of the studies cited indicated that black-white marriages more often involve black men and white women than vice versa. These individuals tend to be older than those who contracted racially endogamous marriages. There is some evidence that these higher ages at marriage are associated with the persons' having been previously married.

Many of these earlier studies suggest that the majority who enter interracial marriages are relatively isolated from their families to begin with. Often, the family and friends of the white spouse did not know of the courtship, which tended to be carried on with some secrecy. In some cases, this clandestincy was continued after marriage.

As to the "social types" who intermarried, some of the blacks were intellectuals, bohemians, members of cults, and lower-class persons without race pride. Among the whites, they were widowed, divorced, older, rural, lower-class, and foreign-born. The assertion that black-white marriages most often involve a prosperous black man and a lower-class white woman has been seriously questioned.

Many couples reported having some difficulties. The problem of being stared at in public places was mentioned by several respondents. Some of the black and white spouses had lost their jobs when employers learned of their marriages; others concealed their marriages from employers and fellow workers.

Some couples were discriminated against in securing housing. As a result, they usually lived in black communities or in peripheral areas. These marriages tended to be accepted by the black, but not by the *white spouses'* relatives and friends. On the other hand, not all of the white spouses' parents and relatives were opposed to such unions. Their friends were more often black than white; relatively few had extensive contacts with other interracially married couples. In general, the problems encountered by interracial couples were those typically met by Negro couples.

Most of the couples had children. Relatively little discrimination against the children was generated from Negroes; but virtually all parents acknowledged that their children would have to be raised as Negroes. Some of the children suffered emotional and social maladjustment. A few solved this dilemma by passing, while others made adjustments in the black community.

Despite the negative attitudes and reactions toward interracial marriages, blacks and whites continue to marry each other. Furthermore, it appears that this trend will persist. In the face of many societal pressures, why, then, do these marriages continue to occur? This question is examined in Chapter 4.

3

Methodology and Data

THIS CHAPTER GIVES a brief description of some demographic features of the metropolitan areas in which mixed couples reside. Secondly, it discusses the sample and its social characteristics, interviewing procedures, analysis of the data, and limitations of the study.

This research follows the basic principle and method ordinarily employed in social anthropology. Data-gathering techniques used include in-depth taped interviews, participant observation, and the use of informants. The field work on which this inquiry is based was conducted in two Midwestern and two Southern cities. These are Champaign-Urbana, Illinois; Cambridge, Ohio; Birmingham, Alabama; and Jackson, Mississippi. It was carried out in two phases—the first in Champaign-Urbana from September 1970 to June 1971, and the second in the remaining three cities from December 1972 to April 1974.

THE PHYSICAL SETTINGS

Champaign-Urbana is one community made up of two municipalities with a total estimated population of 163,281 of which 12,943 or 8 percent are black.[1] Wright Street runs north and south through the University of Illinois campus area, dividing Champaign and Urbana. This community is approximately 130 miles southwest of Chicago and ninety-six miles northeast of Springfield (the capital of Illinois). The principal social and economic factor in the life of this town, however, is the University of Illinois, which employs about 5,000 faculty and staff members. The university also has an enrollment of approximately 30,000 students who make use of many services of the twin cities.

Apart from the university, the major economic interests are those of retail business and real estate. Generally, commercial and real estate entrepreneurs constitute the indigenous elite. Moreover, attorneys, physicians, and professionals from the university dominate the political and social life of the community.[2]

Cambridge, Ohio, is approximately ninety miles east of Columbus. It is located on the world's largest interchange— i.e., Interstate 70 and 77. Its 1970 estimated population was 13,656 with 543 of these residents or 4 percent being black.[3] Some of the city's major industrial products are plastics, chemicals, various and sundry kinds of electrical appliances, and cash registers.

Birmingham is in the north central part of the state of Alabama. Its total population is approximately 739,274 of which 217,303 or 29 percent are black.[4] This metropolis experienced rapid development as an industrial center throughout the twentieth century. All materials needed for making steel are found in close proximity, and the industrial development of the city is based largely on immense mineral deposits. Pig iron and steel have always been the city's leading products. Among some of the other important products are cast iron (60 percent of the national supply of pressure pipes), aircraft, steel cars, rails, stoves, cotton gins, machinery for coal mining, brick, cement, corn meal, textiles, chemicals, meat products, and explosives. Birmingham's educational facilities include seven major colleges and/or universities, and several smaller educational facilities.[5]

The capital of Mississippi, Jackson is on the Pearl River about thirty-five miles southwest of the center of the state. The total population of this city is 258,906 of which 96,418 or 37.2 percent are black.[6] During and after World War II, Jackson's growth was phenomenal. Formerly a white-collar city, it began to attract industries but wisely avoided the evil of industrial slums. Its wide streets, modern skyscrapers, and smoke-free air give it the clean and spacious appearance of a Western city. Major industrial items are glass, tile, cans, textiles, electronic equipment, and meat and dairy products. Jackson's educational facilities include five colleges, a law school, a school of medicine and nursing, and an evening division of the University of Mississippi.[7]

Generally speaking, these four municipalities are typical American cities. The residents are no different from the average American. They are born in families, socialized to internalize certain social, religious, and political values and beliefs, proceed through the various developmental stages of growth, get married, procreate, rear their children, and spend the bulk of their waking hours earning a livelihood. For the most part, the endogamous marriage norms therefore are stringently adhered to, and a violation thereof provokes negative reactions.

SAMPLE CHARACTERISTICS

Gordon states that interracial marriages are those in which the parties to the marriage belong to different races. Even though a Negro Protestant may marry a white Protestant, their marriage will correctly be regarded as interracial. Persons of different ethnic stock and color, no matter what their religion or national origin, will remain members of different races. Such marriages will nearly always be termed interracial.[8] The terms *interracial, intermarried,* and *mixed marriages* will be used interchangeably throughout this book to refer to black-white marriages.

Information pertinent to the names and places of residence of those who have married interracially is difficult to obtain.

One reason is that in many areas, recent legislation prohibits the designation of race on marriage licenses. Even where it is not illegal, oftentimes this information is not available to the public.

No attempt was made to select families either on the basis of social class characteristics (such as occupation, education, income) or whether the marriage was successful or unsuccessful. The basic criteria for selection were that the couples be black-white, legally married, and willing to grant an interview. A total of sixty-seven families were contacted (for participation in the study) in the four cities. At least 95 percent of these were made known to me by informants. Only forty of the families, however, agreed to an interview. Tables 3-1 and

Table 3–1
Location and Number of Couples Contacted

| Location | Total | Number Contacted | |
		Black male– white female	White male– black female
Champaign-Urbana, Illinois	31	25	6
Cambridge, Ohio	20	19	1
Birmingham, Alabama	11	9	2
Jackson, Mississippi	5	4	1
Totals	67	57	10

3-2 indicate the number of couples contacted, marital combination, residential location, and the actual number who granted interviews.

Birthplaces of the Respondents

Fourteen of the black males were born in the South; seventeen in the Midwest; and the remaining two in New York, and Oregon. The seven white males were born in Illinois-2, Massachusetts-2, Ohio, Africa, and Germany. The seven black females were born in Alabama-2, Georgia, Ohio, Illinois, Massachusetts, and Texas. Five of the white females were born in

Table 3–2
Location and Number of Couples Who Granted Interviews

Location	Total	Number Granting Interviews	
		Black male–white female	White male–black female
Champaign-Urbana, Illinois*	20	16	4
Cambridge, Ohio	11	10	1
Birmingham, Alabama	7	5	2
Jackson, Mississippi	2	2	0
Totals	40	33	7

*Aside from those contacted, there were many more married couples and several regular and irregular unions (of cohabitation) known to live in this area. Contacts were also made with a few couples in Washington, D.C.; New Orleans, Louisiana; Atlanta, Georgia; and Tuskegee, Alabama. However, time, limited financial resources, and the difficulties involved in convincing these individuals as to the real intent of this research and in simply setting up appointments resulted in a relatively small sample.

Alabama; eleven in Ohio; eight in Illinois; three in Massachusetts; two in Michigan; and the remaining four in New York, Indiana, England, and Germany.

Ages, and Length of Courtship and Marriage

Age at marriage in the United States has been declining for both men and women for the past century. Around 1890, the median age for grooms was 26.0 and for brides 22.0. Corresponding figures at the present time are 22.5 for men and, 20.5 for women.[9]

The median age at marriage for the grooms in this investigation was 27.5; for the brides, 21.0. The mean age at marriage for the total sample is 24.3. The current mean age for the group as a whole is 29.7. This was the second marriage for eight of the black grooms, two of the black brides, and five of the white brides. They dated for a mean number of 15.9 months. The sample as a whole has been married for a mean number of 5.4 years. Twenty-six of the couples have been married from one to four years; five, for seven years; four, from nine to twelve years; two for fourteen; one, sixteen; and two for nineteen and twenty-one respectively. Two of the female spouses were separated (not divorced) from their husbands. Table 3-3 reports the general characteristics of the sample.

It is apparent that the median age for these grooms who are mostly blacks is higher than that for the general population. On the other hand, however, the median age for the brides is about the same as that for the country as a whole. This indicates a slight decrease in the median age at marriage for these black-white couples as compared to the Philadelphia sample,[10] which had a median age of twenty-eight for all spouses. The same holds true for the Los Angeles couples which had a median age of thirty-nine for the white spouses. The median age of the Indiana sample was slightly lower than the Philadelphia and Los Angeles groups, but much higher than that of the general population.[12] This decrease in the median age suggests than that these marriages are becoming more and more similar to those of persons who marry within their own racial group—which is to say, they are becoming more socially and educationally homogamous, despite the race of the constituents. Moreover, a lower median age might be due to a smaller proportion of second or remarriages in this sample, as compared with other studies. Due to the small size of the sample, any conclusion drawn as to whether these marriages are becoming more similar to those of the general population is in part speculative.

Ages and Residence of the Children

There is a total of seventy-two children in these families. Five are all white in that they are the products of previous white-white marriages. Of this group, four of these children presently live with their mothers and black stepfathers; and one child lives with his mother's relatives. Two of the five all black children reside with their mother and white stepfather,

Table 3–3
Social Characteristics of the Sample

General Attributes	Summary Description
Number of families studied	
Black male–white female	33
White male–black female	7
Number of couples living together at time of study	38
Mean age of respondents	29.7
Mean number of months dated	15.9
Mean number of years married	5.4
Mean age at present marriage	24.3
Number of couples both in their second marriage	3
Number of respondents in their second marriage	15
Children	
All black	5
All white	5
Mulatto	62
Mean age	7.1
Mean number per family	1.8
Childless couples	11
Religious preference of the respondents at time of study	
Protestant	35
Catholic	9
Jewish	1
Baha'i	2
None	33
Education	
Less than high school	15
4 years of high school	28
1–3 years of college	21
4 or more years of college	16
Occupational description	
Professional and technical workers	18
Managers and proprietors	1
Clerical and sales workers	16
Craftsmen and foremen	3
Semiskilled and unskilled workers	16
Students	3
Housewives	21
Unknown	2

and three with their father and white stepmother. Twenty-seven range in age from nine months to six-and-one-half years, with more than 50 percent below the age of five. Ten range from eight to twelve years of age, and one was fifteen. Of the sixty-two mulatto children, in my opinion, seventeen could actually pass for white.

Education

Five of the black grooms hold the bachelor's degree or above. Seven have completed one to three years of college; eight hold high school diplomas; and the remaining thirteen have less than a high school education. Three of the white grooms have completed four and more years of college; and two, from one to three years. One holds a high school diploma, and one did not complete high school.

Of the white brides, six possess the bachelor's degree or above; seven completed one to three years of college; thirteen completed high school; and seven did not finish. Two of the black brides have four or more years of college; two, from one to three years; one completed, and two did not finish high school.

Occupations

The occupations of the black grooms are as follows: probation officer, teacher, musician, photographer-reporter, director of plays and freelance writer, counselor, cameraman at a television station, assistant director of a poverty program, salesman, craftsmen (three work in the building trades), auto-body repairer, journeyman, aircraft mechanic, and student (2). The job title of one is unknown, and the remainder work in semiskilled and unskilled occupations.

Four of the white brides are teachers; four are secretaries, one works in a Head Start program, one is a salesclerk, eleven are semiskilled workers, and twelve are housewives. (Two are on the AFDC program—Aid to Families with Dependent Children.)

One of the white grooms is a university professor, one is a computer programmer, one is a graduate student, and three are semiskilled laborers. The occupation of one is unknown. On the other hand, one of the black brides is a university professor; one, a computer programmer; one, a nurse; one, a secretary; and two, housewives (of which one is on the AFDC program).

Religious Affiliation

Five of the families are actively associated with the church —four Protestant, the other Baha'i. However, before their present marriage, most of them were Protestants. Five are of the Catholic faith. One respondent was Jewish. After marriage, the couples tended to sever ties with their religious organizations. Thirty-three of the respondents report no preference for religion. Moreover, an overwhelming, majority do not hold membership in other organizations. Some express the view that they are antiorganizational.

Household Composition

The most prevalant household arrangement (thirty-five families) is the nuclear family type—consisting of father, mother, and offspring. There are two households consisting of two interracially married families each (including children). The apparent reasons for this are grounded in economics and a need for companionship. One other household is composed of a black husband's family of orientation and of course his family of procreation.

INTERVIEWING PROCEDURES

The initial contact with a family was either made by telephone or through an introduction by an informant. I anticipated that after meeting with a few respondents, they would be able to provide information on other couples—as to who they are and where they live. This, surprisingly, was not the case. With the exception of the Cambridge sample, a majority had no knowledge of the existence of other black-white couples in their areas.

Many of the persons contacted expressed (save the Cambridge group) strong opposition toward participation in this investigation. Some of the reasons given for refusals were: "We have been through this too many times already." "I don't want to be bothered." "I don't have anything to say about it." "I will not subject my children to this type of thing anymore." Implicit in some of the reactions was the idea that their private lives were being invaded. As one individual put it, "I have read about that stuff, but I am not interested in discussing it with anyone." After explaining to another potential respondent my desire to interview her family, the indignant reply was: "You don't have any questions to ask me because I am not answering any." According to reports from a few informants in the Champaign-Urbana area, a partial explanation for some refusals is that some of the couples were allegedly having marital problems which I assume they did not care to discuss. On the other hand, many of those who agreed to an interview were quite enthusiastic about relating much of their experience.

The same questions were asked of each family, with modifications as the special circumstances required. With the exception of two families, husbands and wives were always interviewed together. It is unknown as to what extent this arrangement influenced their responses. The information reported might possibly have been somewhat different had husband and wife been interviewed separately. Usually, if the couples had children, they were also present. The interviews were semistructured in that they allowed the respondents full liberty to formulate their answers and freely express themselves. Considering the limitations and biases of informants, extensive use was also made of several long-time residents in the various communities to obtain information regarding general lifestyles of black-white couples.

The interviews, which usually took place in the family's living room, were in each instance tape-recorded and transcribed, thereby retaining the actual phraseology, feelings, emotions, tones of voice, and specific statements of those being questioned. The transcriptions of the interviews were rearranged and edited to obliterate the identity of any family.

The range of experiences and the interests expressed by the respondents usually determined the length of the interviews. The sessions however, lasted from one to four hours—averaging about one and one-half hours per family. However, much more time was spent before and after the taping. In reference to the Champaign-Urbana sample, many additional home visits were made; and in many cases, follow-up phone calls were necessary in order to ascertain other important information. For the most part, the interviews were conducted during nonrush hours—usually on weekends and holidays from 1 to 5 P.M., or 7 to 11:30 P.M. weekdays.

The Cambridge sample was quite disposed to discuss their marriage and family life. Of the twenty persons contacted, not a single one refused to be interviewed. They were open and somewhat enthusiastic about the whole thing. The problem here basically involved time. It was difficult to interview this number of families in a two or three day period. Doing so required that a researcher remain in the area long enough to schedule appointments at the convenience of the respondents.

Unlike the above group, the Birmingham sample was much more reluctant to participate. This apparent apprehension is probably related to their living in the Southern region of the country. Without question, there is a much greater aversion toward black-white marriages in the South than in other areas of the country. Despite the relative large size and urban nature of Birmingham, Alabama, and Jackson, Mississippi, it is obvious that black-white couples in these cities feel much more inhibited in their activities than exemplified by the Champaign-Urbana and Cambridge samples. Out of the five contacts made in Jackson, only two granted interviews. I would venture to say that the general attitude there is similar to that of the Birmingham group.

Analysis of Data

Conclusions will be drawn on the basis of a comparison of the findings of this study with those of earlier investigations. Hopefully this approach will enable us to determine whether or not the life patterns and personal experiences of black-white couples in the 1970s differ drastically from what they did one, two, or three decades ago.

In a heterogeneous society where many aspects of family organization are becoming more and more questionable, a study of this nature might reveal important indications on which predictions can be made about family forms in the distant future. Also, many persons might be interested in knowing what ultimate effect of interracial marriage might have upon the American kinship structure; and what type of religious, social class, cultural, ethnic, and regional problems, if any, might be anticipated.

Limitations of the Study

As no attempt was made to draw a representative sample of black-white marriages, conclusions and inferences from the present study should not be interpreted as applying to the total black-white married population of the United States. A second limitation inheres in the fact that in view of certain circumstances, it was unwise to interview husband and wife separately. Had separate interviews been held, it is possible that the responses reported here might reflect some variation.

One of the problems involved in the interview is that it is not a conversation in the usual sense. In addition, not allowing the respondent much freedom to choose what will be discussed, the interviewer frequently enters the encounter with different perspectives from those of the subject.[13] George H. Mead points out that the process of answering questions is a social act which means that the respondent is reacting to a total situation and not just to the question, which in some cases could certainly influence the content of a statement.[14] A further limitation is that despite the efforts to be totally objective, a researcher is not completely free of values and biases which at times might possibly seep into his analysis.

These conditions are sufficient to suggest that the result of a study free of some of these methodological problems might vary somewhat from those reported here.

4

Motives for Black-White Marriages

ONE PLAUSIBLE EXPLANATION for the prohibition of racial-caste intermarriage in the United States lies in the structural and functional elements of the system, according to Robert K. Merton. The taboo, he says, seems to be largely supported by the standardized sentiments of both blacks and whites, and consequently, the rate of intermarriage continues to be low. What then, he asks, are the motives for racial intermarriages which occur in spite of the taboo?[1] This chapter examines some of the motives for intermarriage. First, it explores various interpretations found in the literature; and second, a discussion follows concerning motives as reported by the forty couples.

SOME EXPLANATIONS FOR MIXED MARRIAGES

Several theories have been proposed in an effort to explain marriage across racial lines. The notion that those who contract mixed marriages are somehow different from the rest of the population finds reinforcement in both popular and professional circles. However, the degree of nonconformity ascribed to the intermarried varies considerably from being very mild to strong. Consider the statement attributed to psychiatrist Thomas Brayboy (a black himself) that "deep seated psychological sickness of various sorts underlie the 'vast majority' of marriages between blacks and whites." Brayboy goes on to say that "the participants in such marital unions often make use of the 'unique opportunity' that socially opposed or forbidden interracial sex offers for 'acting out' their personal problems." Thus, he observed, "these marriages often have little to do with love and tenderness; instead, they are arenas for hostility, control and revenge."[2]

Another explanation advanced is that some whites may marry nonwhites for idealistic or liberal reasons—i.e., to defy the prevalent cultural prejudice of the society. Intermarrying then demonstrates refusal to identify with racial bigotry.[3]

A third motive might be repudiation. Ruth S. Cavan asserts that a mixed marriage "indicates that the person either has not been thoroughly integrated into his social group or has repudiated it for some reason. His needs are not met there; he seeks elsewhere for contacts, friendship, and marriage."[4] He may feel like a misfit; he may have been rejected; and he is therefore manifesting a mutual rejection by overstepping the bounds of one of his group's strongest norms.[5] He tends to be either somewhat disorganized or a cosmopolitan person who makes friendships on a personal rather than a cultural basis.[6]

There is also the notion that a white person may marry a nonwhite to rebel against parental authority. This desire to hurt the parents may be conscious or unconscious; and thus it appears to be one of the principal motivations for interracial marriage (or even dating) among many young white Americans of the middle class.[7]

The idea of neurotic self-hate or self-degradation (by marriage to an "inferior") also finds reinforcement in some circles. Richard L. Rubenstein described a Radcliffe girl of Protestant background who became pregnant by two successive Jewish boys. He noted that she was strongly ambivalent toward Jews:

> Women frequently enter such relationships in order to degrade themselves and their families. Similar mechanisms are often at work in liaisons between white women and

Negro men. As the need for self-degradation wore out, resentment against the husband as the imagined source of
degradation could create a host of thoroughly unpleasant
situations.[8]

Still another reason offered is the "lure of the exotic."
This syndrome may induce a person to be attracted to and
marry someone other than a member of his or her own racial
group. The individual may experience a profound psycho-
sexual attraction to the "otherness" of someone who may be
physically different. The existence and repercussions of this
kind of attraction are described in the folklore and literature of
many ancient and modern cultures.

The inherent problem with most of these conceptual notions as motives for out-marriage is that they are too unsystem-
atic, fragmentary, and often speculative. In many instances
they are derived on the basis of individual cases or small samples. Such data are not easily measured. Information then,
gathered in such a manner should not be accepted as valid
reasons for all mixed marriages.

When one looks at the other side of the coin, many interracial marriages occur for the simple reason that the individuals are in love. In this case, there is no motivational difference between an interracial and intraracial marriage. Though
some of these factors might be in operation, all of the above
"motivations" are not necessarily involved in out-marriage. It
is likely that most black-white couples marry for precisely the
same reasons that racially similar couples do. The fact that
such an alliance is formed in the first place may indicate a
high degree of motivation on the part of both partners. The
couple's compatibility may be so unusually high in comparison to those of the same race, that the marriage may succeed
despite the social context in which it takes place.[9] This brief
exposition of a hodgepodge of explanations still leaves the basic question unanswered; and that is: what are the real reasons
for marrying interracially in contemporary American society?
These are explored next.

Motives as Reported by the Respondents

In the past, black-white couples generally became acquainted through occupational contacts, mutual friends, or shared neighborhoods. Desegregation of many areas of social and public life has greatly facilitated these contacts. In view of the multitude of changes which have occurred within the last decade, the bases for black-white marriages in the 1970s have drastically shifted from what they were one, two, or three decades ago.

For all practical purposes, motives for marriage as given by the respondents (in the present study) are classified into three general categories. These are: (1) nonrace-related, (2) race-related, and (3) the marginal status of an individual in his racial group. Although these categories are mutually exclusive, motives for marriage are not. Moreover, many of the spouses reported a combination of reasons for marriage.

In relation to nonrace-related motives, a majority of the respondents reported "love" (attraction, attachment, affection) and compatibility as their basic reasons for marriage. In addition to these two factors, one each of the black and white brides listed pregnancy as a possible cause. Nine of the black grooms, two white brides, and one white groom indicated race-related reasons. Of this number, three of the black males view their marital behavior in part as a rebellion against society. Four of these men also perceive the white female as less domineering than the black female—which was a decisive factor for their entering a marriage of this type. One of the white grooms was extremely impressed with the "independent and self-sufficient qualities exemplified by the black female."

Two black grooms also conceptualize the white female as a status symbol. An explanation advanced by two of the white brides (for marrying blacks) is that a person of the opposite race is more appealing and interesting.

Some of the motives stated are related to the marginal

status of the individual in his or her racial group. For example, two of the black brides who hold graduate degrees reported that the desire to marry a person of comparable educational-occupational status narrowed their field of blacks who were eligible as marriage partners. This in turn stimulated their interest to marry whites. Moreover, one of the white brides who is in her second interracial marriage reported that once a white girl crosses the color line and especially if she has children, it is difficult for her to return to white society and be accepted. Table 4-1 indicates the number of respondents who specifically mentioned different motives for marriage.

The remainder of this chapter describes some of the reasons these individuals decided to marry. The first section is concerned with nonrace-related causes. Secondly, emphasis is focused on race-related reasons. Finally, an examination of the relationship between a person having a marginal status and his marrying interracially is included.

There is no attempt to include specific data from each couple; but instead one, two, or three interviews germane to each category are utilized to illustrate the various reasons. The interviews presented are selected not because they are more interesting than some of the others, but instead, because they appear to be representative of the motives indicated in a given category.

NONRACE-RELATED MOTIVES

According to Robert O. Blood, Jr., black-white marriages are the least intrinsically incompatible of all mixed marriages for these individuals are similar in terms of culture and religion. Then what is there to differentiate them except physical appearance? It stands to reason then that persons color-blind enough to cross the color bar are unlikely to find that "bar" dividing them, provided they are similar in other respects.[10] For most of these couples, race was not an important factor in mate selection.

Table 4–1
Number of Respondents Who Mentioned Specific
Motives for Their Marriage

| | Race and Sex of Spouse | | | |
Motives	Black male	Black female	White male	White female
Nonrace-related motives				
Love	28	12	6	25
Compatibility	28	12	6	25
Pregnancy		1		1
Race-related motives				
Other race more appealing, interesting				2
Rebellion against society	3			
White female a "status symbol"	2			
White female less domineering	4			
Black female more independent, self-sufficient			1	
Marginality				
Desire for a husband of comparable educational-occupational status		2		
Ostracized from one's own racial group				1

Although these categories are mutually exclusive, motives for marriage are not. Some of the respondents indicated a combination of reasons for marriage.

Love and Compatibility

Many persons ascribe deviant social and psychological characteristics to an individual who marries outside his or her race; for he or she supposedly suffers from a deep-seated psychological sickness. Yet, there is little evidence to support this argument. The results of this survey strongly suggest that a majority of interracial dating and marriage is not related to some pathological abnormality or to any crusade against prejudice. Table 4-2 lists combinations of motives as asserted by husband and wife. Grounds for interracial marriages are usually the same as those for marriage between persons of the same race. For example, thirty-one of these couples cited love and compatibility as their primary motives for getting married. Seven other couples mentioned these factors among other reasons. Most of them reported that their initial relationships were based on shared interests, ideas, and values. The following is a case in point.

One day, while having lunch at a sandwich shop, Dave decided to bet his friend that he could "lay" Rose (a white waitress working there). He approached her with the story: "My cousin wants to meet you." Immediately, she concluded that his friend (who was white) was not his cousin. As the conversation progressed, she complimented Dave on his "good looking car." He then extended her an invitation to ride which she accepted.

Later, Rose told her mother what had transpired and asked permission to date this black man. At first, her mother consented because she felt that Rose was more or less joking; but when she learned that her daughter was serious, she then said no! Dave continued to frequent the sandwich shop and for a while, Rose attempted to avoid him out of fear that not to do so would create conflict with her mother. On one occasion, she even requested that the manager tell Dave that he was wasting his time and to stop harassing her. Dave's reply was: "I have heard that before." Finally she agreed to a date in order to explain that she could not establish such an acquaintance because of the problems it would create with her mother. But they detected a mutual interest and continued to date, without the mother's knowing.

After about six months, this romance eventually generated turmoil between the mother and daughter which resulted in Rose's leaving home. At this time she was only seventeen. A few days later however, she called her mother and said she was coming home. Dave accompanied her; and when they arrived, the police were there. He was not arrested because he did not lure Rose away from home; she left on her own accord.

Despite the mother's negative attitude, they continued to

Table 4–2
Motives for Marriage Among Black-White Couples

Motives	Marital Combination	
	Black male-white female	White male-black female
Love and compatibility only	28	3
Love, compatibility and other motives		
1. H—Rebellion, and white female less domineering W—Love—compatibility	1	
2. H—Rebellion, and white female a status symbol W—Love—compatibility	1	
3. H—Love—compatibility W—Love—compatibility, and pregnancy	1	2
4. H—Independency, self-sufficiency, and love—compatibility W—Love—compatibility, and a desire to marry a person of comparable educational-occupational status		1
5. H—Love—compatibility W—Love—compatibility, and a desire to marry a person of comparable educational-occupational status		1
Other combinations of motives (excluding love—compatibility)		
1. H—Rebellion, and white female less domineering W—Other race more appealing—interesting	1	
2. H—White female a status symbol W—Ostracized from own racial group	1	

H = Husband
W = Wife

see each other and eventually became engaged. Rose then moved to Champaign but encountered difficulty in transferring to another high school. In order to complete high school, Rose commuted to her hometown. After graduation and her eighteenth birthday, they were wed. Rose married Dave because "he is a good person." She loves him and is proud to be with him.

Dave thinks of Rose "as being a warm and considerate individual who cares about other people" which he considers a wonderful way to be. He is positive that he did not marry her because she is white and an alleged status symbol for a black man. Rose had lived in an all white community all her life, and had never encountered undesirable racial experiences or been involved in meaningful discussions pertinent to race.

This suggests that at least for Rose and Dave, race might not have been one of the most salient attributes of mate selection. Perhaps an hypothesis might be suggested here that for some people, racial categories in mate selection are not salient. However, to say that nonsalience is currently the basis for black-white marriages at this time is indeed ludicrous. Further evidence for this hypothesis is found in the cases of couples A and B.

COUPLE A

Husband: I never thought of Sarah as being black. She's a nice person. I always look at her as a human being.

Wife: I never really thought I was marrying a white person as such. He's just Harry. We felt we were good for each other, so we got married.

COUPLE B

Husband: There was no real motivation on my part. If you can understand a person, you can learn to care about that person. Love and understanding makes one marry; not just the color of one's skin. I guess I was in love.

Wife: The color didn't have anything to do with it. I was in love with the person and not with the color. That's all there was to it. I was never taught prejudice in my home. I've never had bad feelings against Negroes.

Here again, couples reported that race was an insignificant consideration in their decision to marry. They perceive their relationship as developing out of common interests and values.

As mentioned earlier, this type of motivation was not at all uncommon among this group. Another couple that fits a similar description met at a general hospital where they worked. The white wife relates some of her experiences which eventually led to marriage.

> When we first started going together (in February), we were like brother and sister. He had no romantic inclination about . . . he has a sense of humor and I do too . . . we would have everybody on the receiving ward cracking up . . . we would go to . . . a bookshop and restaurant . . . to the opera sometimes . . . but really not as a date. It was always a spur-of-the-moment thing. . . . We would get off (work) at seven A.M. and go have breakfast together. We were really friends. He'd tell me all his love problems and I'd tell him all mine. I really liked him; but I wasn't sure how much he cared about me. He never even tried to kiss me, or anything; so, I thought maybe he did not really like girls, maybe he likes fellows, and that he was just handing me that crap. I really thought that. I liked him better than any fellow I knew. He was more adult. We became lovers. . . . I found out he didn't like boys. In August I told him I loved him. Between August and September, he got rid of his other three girls, and then it was just he and I.

Most of these marital relationships are characterized by an intense degree of mutual interests, ideas, and values. However, in the above case, there are other elements that might have played a vital role. First, this is the second marriage for the bride. Second, she has two children by her first husband. This possibly places some limitations on her field of eligibles. Third, Joyce also frequented the home of another black-white married couple who worked at the same hospital. These conditions more than likely had some bearing on her decision to date a black man in the first place. But on the other hand, their situation is no different from those of the general population.

In this connection, the idea of the companionship family, says Farber, is that individuals seek personal happiness, adjustment, and freedom within the family setting. This type of family is based in contemporary society.[11] Farber further adds, in a society in which the trend is also toward permanent availability (i.e., if things do not work out, the couple may divorce and try again), mutual enjoyment, interests, and congeniality of goals appear to override categorical distinctions in the United States selection process. As homogamy then based upon traditional categories (race, religion, social class) declines, homogamy based on personal characteristics can be expected to become the primary factor in mate selection.[12] Regarding the participants in this survey, in a majority of the cases, these factors certainly seemed to have outweighed racial considerations. However, isolated cases involving "deviant" motivations and/or attitudes do exist—an issue to which I now turn.

Pregnancy

A contributing factor influencing one couple to get married was pregnancy. Even though this couple said they were "deeply in love," pregnancy was a major consideration. Steve and Betty met on a blind date arranged by Betty's sister. Betty had recently come to Boston and did not enjoy staying home alone while her sister, Hane, went out; so she decided to go out with Steve despite her knowing he was black. Moreover, "a person's race does not really matter to me. I don't think in terms of color. I never really thought about it that much." Betty continued to date Steve primarily because she doubledated with her sister, and three months after the romance began, the two were married.

Her parents did not know about the courtship until about a month before the marriage. She told them after she became pregnant. However, at this time, they did not know Steve was black. Betty decided to write a "long letter and inform them." She reports the reactions of her parents:

> They acted very good about it. I thought they were going to be upset; they really surprised me. I thought because they were living in a small community . . . they didn't know about interracial couples. My parents obviously aren't prejudiced; but most people in small towns don't think of themselves as being so; and I just thought maybe my parents were; but they are not. They love him. They didn't really care whether he was black or white; they were just glad that he was a good person.

Steve, like his wife, who is a teacher-musician, is from a middle-class family background. His mother is a nurse and his father is deceased. Betty holds a bachelor's degree. Her father is an electrical research engineer, and her mother is a secretary. Since both individuals are from a middle-class family background, it is likely that they have common interests and ideals. As one respondent puts it: "One thinks only of the person whom he or she is marrying, and not the race as a whole."

The case further suggests that race (for this couple) appears not to have been a salient characteristic. However, the question that comes to mind is: Would the marriage have occurred had not Betty become pregnant? This question is difficult to answer. It was pointed out that the possibility of their living together had been discussed and agreed upon before she became pregnant. Steve states that: "So evidently since the two of us had agreed to live together, we were thinking about the possibility of getting married anyway. So it's possible that it would have happened anyway" (i.e., getting married).

Pregnancy certainly cannot be ignored as a precipitating reason to contract this union. On the other hand, maybe marrying a person of a different race did not really matter to these individuals.

RACE-RELATED MOTIVES

Many of the reasons for marriage imply racial overtones in that it appears that some underlying prejudicial motivation partially accounts for some of these individuals initiating marriage oriented relationships. To a large degree, these feelings are generated by the psychic makeup of the social structure itself. Some of these motivations which have been alluded to earlier are: (1) the other race is more appealing and interesting; (2) some people want to strike out, rebel, or get even with society for its injustices; (3) the white female is viewed by some as a status symbol; (4) the white female is far less domineering than her black counterpart; and (5) the black female is far more independent and self-sufficient than the white female. In addition to love, compatibility, and pregnancy, some of the above reasons were given by six of the spouses as influencing them to marry. This section provides a discussion of these race-related causes as specifically mentioned by some of the respondents.

Other Race More Appealing

The notion that "opposites attract" impels some individuals to contract a marriage. For example, one of the white brides who says she has never dated men of her own race commented that "white men simply do not appeal to me." A second white bride reported a similar inclination:

> I have never dated white men. They do not appeal to me. Black men are more passionate. They rap better—dance better—and get more involved than white dudes. With white dudes, it seems like an "on the surface" thing.

In some regards, another white bride suggested that she was in part stimulated to date interracially because she was somewhat fascinated by a black man's "rap," his "line"—i.e., the ways he talks while at the same time using certain mannerisms.

> The difference that I noticed at first was a black man's rap. You can really be super ugly, but he will make you feel like you are beautiful. It's the way he handles himself. He has more confidence in himself. He might not really be that cool. On the inside, he might really be insecure; but on the outside, everybody will say: "Wow, he's super cool."
> Also, at work, there are lots of white chicks that really

dig on black men, but they don't want anybody to know it. But I have always been open about it. Even when we first started dating, I never tried to hide it. I think a lot of those women . . . if they really like black men, they are afraid someone will find it out . . . so they hide, they sneak.

In reference to this same point, it is the opinion of one of the couples that some people have sexual hang-ups in that they are sexually stimulated by members of the opposite race. For example, this black bride reports that "some black men believe that a pink vagina is simply better." The groom added that for some persons there is a similar feeling about the great black vagina or the great black stallion. They both pointed out that this attitude regarding the sexual superiority of the other race exists among many blacks and whites. They described one of their white male friends as "having a sexual sensation for black women." The wife says that "he is crazy about black women. He even tried to talk to me once; and I told him to just get away from me; for if sex was his reason, I wasn't interested."

Much of this alleged sexual propensity is partially accounted for by the unfamiliarity. This means that some individuals are sexually curious about those with whom they have not had sexual contacts—especially (if for some) this act is taboo or forbidden. This serves only to intensify this curiosity. This attitude was quite pronounced and probably still is to some degree, among American soldiers (particularly Southern blacks) in foreign countries. For example, in the late 1950s during my European military duty, one of the first goals a Southern black male had to accomplish was to have sex with a white woman. After this act was repeatedly done, the intense curiosity and desire soon dissipated. And later many of these men actually admitted that it was quite absurd and immature for people to have such wild and bizarre ideas about sex. For then they realized that women were women, and men were men; and for a majority of them, being intrigued over skin color was no longer pronounced. In fact, after associating with white females for a long period of time and not having any contact with black women, many of these black males then began to express a strong sexual desire for black women, which indicated a developing curiosity in the opposite direction.

To a lesser extent, this same type behavior was manifested by many white soldiers. I recall a black Wac (a member of the Women's Army Corps) being stationed in the same area who had more white male "callers" than she could accommodate. This can partially be explained by the fact that she was the only black woman in the vicinity. It may sound strange but anytime she would go out on dates, white men would cluster around her like "bees on a hive." There were always six to eight men in her presence—presumably competing for her attention. I would judge that this is a reflection of that same "sexual curiosity," exemplified by the black men. The cliche: "Once the prize being pursued is achieved, then the novelty wears off," adequately sums up this phenomenon. Here again, the situation boils down to the simple fact of man and woman acting out basic human desires, emotions, and needs.

William H. Grier and Price M. Cobbs make the point that in cases where a black-white relationship progresses to marriage, the problems increase exponentially, since in this culture marriage progressively downgrades the importance of the sexual act and lays increasing emphasis on the economic and social functioning of the partners.[13] It is unfortunate that for some of us, it is during the latter phases of the game when we are finally able to "pierce through the trees and view the forest." Albeit, for others, we never reach this point.

Rebellion Against Society

The idea of striking back or getting even with white society through the white woman may initially be a significant factor for some black males desiring to marry white females. One respondent provides a striking example:

> My real reason for wanting a white woman was deep-
> seated. It probably sprang from the inferior feelings I had

from being black. But the total society created these feelings.

On the other hand, this couple's marriage was also flavored by compatibility. The wife comments that "he was good for me in a lot of ways. He had a lot of qualities I liked; and it just worked out . . . beautifully."

A similar view was also expressed by another black husband. Joey reported that at about age eight, he developed a deep-seated hatred for white men as a result of a white Southern plantation owner kicking his pregnant aunt in the stomach because she wasn't picking enough cotton. The aunt and the fetus died. He expresses his feelings:

> This man murdered my aunt. That might be part of the reason I don't care nothing about them, or care to work for them. But if you want some dough, you got to work for them. White women ain't done nothing to no nigger—really. It's them old damn men. They will do anything to you—including hanging your ass from a tree. That is why I don't like them right now—because they don't give a fuck about you. And they don't give a fuck about me being married to this white girl.
>
> All the police around here don't dig me either. I feel they pick on me because of my marriage. I used to fight my black old lady all the time—every week. They didn't say nothing. But if they just see me with this white girl, they want to pick on me. So sometimes I just get them stirred up for the hell of it.

Eldridge Cleaver in his *Soul on Ice* verbalizes his desire to strike out at the system through the white woman. He says that upon his release from prison, he became a rapist.

> Rape was an insurrectionary act. It delighted me that I was defying and trampling upon the white man's law, upon his system of values, and that I was defiling his women—and this point, I believe, was the most satisfying to me because I was very resentful over the historical fact of how the white man has used the black woman. I felt I was getting revenge.[14]

Later however, Cleaver admitted that he was wrong, that he had gone astray—not so much from the white man's law as from being human and civilized. He did not feel justified and therefore lost his pride and self-respect.

It is somewhat apparent that for some black males, vindictiveness seems to be related to the desire to engage in interracial sexual relations. Grier and Cobbs further contend that for some black men, the white woman represents the "socially identified" female ideal and thus an intensely exciting object for his sexual possession. She has been identified as the individual to whom access is barred by every social institution. He might feel a sense of power at having acquired this highly valueable woman and a sense of power that she finds him desirable and indeed that she finds him more desirable than a white lover. But at the same time he perceives her as white and as representative of all the white oppressors who have made his life so wretched.

In possessing the white woman, the black man then has an opportunity to live out murderous fantasies of revenge. He sees himself as degrading her because when she submits to a black lover, she becomes as debased as he. In this way he may feel the gratification of turning the tables on his white oppressor and thus becoming the instrument through which a white person is degraded. While in every other area of life the black man may feel emasculated and humiliated by the white man, here he can reverse the roles and, because of the central importance of the sexual function in human affairs, may feel that the scales are almost balanced.[15]

White Female: A Status Symbol

For some black males, to date or marry interracially is status enhancing. At least two of the black grooms indicated such a response. The following case illustrates this point:

Carol reports that Bob "impressed" her because he was older—so he said. He appeared to be different from the other guys. "He made me feel very special—like a woman. I felt that if we had not got married I would have regretted it for the remainder of my life." Even though this relationship is partly based on attraction and compatibility, implicit are certainly the factors of flaunting a white female, and an attitude of vindictiveness. For example, Bob said that the stares and comments they receive do not bother him; in fact, he enjoys them.

> I enjoy it really. I always like to get myself into other people's minds. This bothers people ... it makes me happy. I just enjoy getting on people's nerves that I don't like.

The Domineering Black Female

There are many pros and cons as to the nature of the black female's personality. She is not infrequently depicted as iron-willed, effectual, treacherous towards, and contemptuous of black men. Many black women have been unlucky in life and love and seek a bitter haven from their disappointments in fanatical self-sufficiency. It is said that still others, out of a tragic fear, brutalize their sons in the child-rearing process, hoping to destroy in them aggressive tendencies which might eventually erupt in assaults against white men and the white system.

These superficial and unbalanced descriptions are predicated on the popular and dangerous myths of *black male emasculation,* and its descendant concept, *black female matriarchy.* In the broad sense, an emasculated people are a broken people who have been reduced to a state of almost total ineffectuality. Their spirit, strength, and vigor have been destroyed. Specifically applied to a male, emasculation connotes the absence of virility and can mean, though not necessarily, effeminacy.

The emasculation theory further alleges that in addition to black men having failed to protect their women and families from racism, they have also failed to develop a foolproof strategy for liberating black people. It is therefore concluded that they are weak and must be brushed aside and overcome by women in the big push toward freedom. This weakness, in part, developed via the route that black women castrated the men by (among other things) playing their economic ace-in-the-hole and complying with their rapists through the use of their bodies to rise on the socioeconomic ladder, leaving black men behind.[16]

Concerning the notion of the "black female matriarchy," E. Franklin Frazier's use of the term *matriarchy*, or what is to-day described by anthropologists and sociologists as *matrifo-cality*, embraces two distinct but interrelated ideas. First, the proportion of female-headed households is significantly higher among lower-class blacks than among lower-class whites. Second, the term *matrifocality* describes a household where the father is present but where the female exercises the dominant influence in family decisions. In Frazier's view, both of these manifestations of matriarchy can be characterized as pathological when compared to the "normal" American family. It should be emphasized that the overwhelming majority of blacks live in two-parent households, but the proportion of female-headed households is about three times that among whites. It should be stressed that middle- and upper-class black families are characteristically patriarchal and that matrifocality is part of the black lower-class subculture.[17]

An examination of the historical vicissitudes of slavery and the role of the black woman and its development as it was influenced by the political and economic organization of American society facilitates an understanding of the "black female matriarchal" phenomenon. Robert Staples feels that family organization of the preslave period of African civilization was a stable patriarchal institution. The ordeal of slavery wrought many changes in this pattern, for the African model in America was an impossibility when the slave's existence was devoted primarily to the cultivation and manufacture of tobacco and cotton. Also the buying and selling of slaves involved the splitting up of families, leaving only the mother-child bond somewhat immune to the disruptive effects of the economic interests of slavery—thus leaving the mother as the prime authority in the household. Moreover, the maintenance of discipline on the plantation prevented husbands and fathers from protecting wives and children against white masters and other more favored slaves. The financial values set on slave children and the rewards given to successful motherhood in cash, kindness, and promotion from field to house slave gave an especially high status to the mother, a status which the father could only enjoy if placed in a position akin to that of a stud animal. Without question, these conditions led to a breaking of family ties and still furthered the degradation of family life. The black family's desire to remain together was subordinated to the interests of the slave-owning class.

Just as in the society at large, power relationships in the family are aligned along economic lines. The power base of the patriarchal family is in large part based on the economic dependence of the female member. In the black slave family, the black woman was independent of the black male for support and assumed a type of leadership in the family life not found in the patriarchal family. At the same time, white society continued to deny black males the opportunity to obtain the economic wherewithal to assume leadership in the family constellation.[18]

Abram Kardiner and Lionel Ovesey suggest that males from female-dominated households generally relate to the mother out of frustrated dependency and hostility. This does not conduce to good relations with the female. It is, therefore consistent with the general hardships of the adaptation of the male that his sex life suffers as a consequence. He fears the female much more than is apparent for intrinsic genetic reasons, and also, because his economic opportunities are worse than the female's. Hence, he is often at the mercy of the woman.[19] In that a large number of black women have had to take the leading role within the family, it is understandable why in many instances, manifestations of dominance prevail.

These companion myths (black male emasculation and black matriarchy) are not recent in their origin; but more recently, they have been popularized by Daniel Patrick Moynihan through his highly publicized and touted work, *The Negro Family: The Case for National Action.* Moynihan's black matriarchy proposition is based, incredibly, on the statistic that *one quarter* of all black families are headed by women. Like most myths, the one of a black matriarchy contains some elements of truth.[20]

There is fragmentary evidence that this factor (i.e., the dominant black female) might partially account for black males' seeking out white females as marital partners. Some black men believe that white females are more affectionate, passive, understanding, and concerned about fulfilling the needs of their husbands. A black female professor, for example, reports that young black men and women often have trouble relating to one another, partly because black women are ready to lash out at black men. One black woman put it this way: "Wow, our mouth. White girls have learned to capitalize on that. We'll use that tongue on you, cut you to pieces."[21]

Four of the black grooms reluctantly agreed with the above position. The remaining thirty-three asserted that to an extent all females (black and white) are domineering. Three of the black husbands actually commented on the issue. Tilman admits that one of his motives for dating and marrying a white girl is that she knows how to treat a man. He compares her with the black female:

> Let a soul brother stay with a soul sister two years and ain't worked none—and see what happens to him. She will put him out. I haven't worked in two years and Ruby hasn't put me out—because she loves me. A soul sister wouldn't take that shit. This woman loves me—loves me to death—well, damn near to death anyway.

It was quite explicit during one of the conversations with a black husband that he shared somewhat similar feelings concerning this point. When he was asked his opinion on this aspect of the black man and woman's relationship, he replied:

> In this town, you don't have too many picks out of black chicks—you know, being pretty, and nice or what you might call fox. They get jealous. And if you get jealous, you get evil. When a black dude starts dating a black chick, and she knows that there are not many black chicks in Cambridge, she thinks she can treat you any way she wants to. So when you get tired of her, you just go somewhere else. You don't have to go through a hassle everytime you take somebody out. Maybe for some black dudes, white girls just turn them on—just does the job.

A third black groom expressed the view that:

> "A personality type" is an individual response determined by particular circumstances. Some black women do tend to be a bit more domineering; the personalities can, however, be molded into what can become a comfortable relationship. The white woman tends to be a little less domineering and responds more to the needs of her man.

It must be emphasized that the above descriptions are not applicable to the majority of black women. Black women, domineering or not, have not had the power in this male-dominated culture to effect a coup against anyone's manhood—in spite of their frequently cited economic "advantage" over the black man. For the duration of their lives, many black women must bear a heavy burden of male frustration and rage through physical abuse, desertions, rejection of their femininity and general appearance. For a black woman to successfully cope with the economic problem often enhances her rejection by black men, or else invites acceptance in the form of exploitation. Stymied in his attempt to protect and free the black woman (and himself), the black man further degrades her. She, doubly powerless and vengeful, insults his manhood by whatever means at her disposal. What this all adds up to is that black men and women are placing ultimate blame for their subjugation on each other, a propensity which fairly reeks of self-hatred. In other words, blacks are still crippled by self-doubt.[22]

Black Female: Independent, Self-Sufficient

Ironically, a domineering personality may be one of the reasons white men seek out black wives. Bill, one of the white husbands, was attracted to Sue, his black wife, by her qualities of dominance, independence, and self-sufficiency. He felt that white women had a need to be dominated.

> They were raised to be servants to their husbands—to please them, sit at home and be pretty. They lack the independence that was forced on black women. . . . I want a wife that is strong—able to run things if necessary, and make decisions on her own. This trait is much more pronounced in black than in white females.

Added to this element, Bill and Sue have shared interests, goals, and values—all of which are educationally oriented. He says they are extremely compatible. "She needs to talk a lot and I'm normally quiet. We complement each other's personalities." Here again, despite the existence of other reasons, love and compatibility continue to flavor these relationships.

MARGINALITY

Although Robert E. Park was probably the first to employ the concept of *the marginal man*, the term has since become largely linked with the name of Everett V. Stonequist. He views the marginal man as an individual who, by virtue of migration, education, marriage, or some other influence, leaves one cultural group without making satisfactory adjustment to another. Accordingly, he finds himself on the margin of each culture but a member of neither.[23] To a degree, this concept partially lends itself to a possible explanation as to why some persons enter a mixed marriage. Three of the respondents could be considered as marginal individuals within our mixed marriage perspective. Two were seeking partners of an equal occupational educational status; and one had been somewhat rejected by her racial group.

A Spouse of Comparable Status

Two of the black wives (who hold graduate degrees) said that they were attracted to the generally higher educational status of white males as compared with black males. There was such a wide gap between their educational achievement and that of the black males they dated that there was very little communication and compatibility. They said that there seemed to be an inverse relationship in the number of school years completed by a black female and her chance of marrying a black man with comparable education or occupation. A case in point follows.

Susan (black) grew up in a black community in Atlanta, Georgia. Her early childhood and adolescent experience was more or less devoid of any close contact with persons other than black. She and Ray met at a Baha'i Center (a religious group) in September 1964. In November, they decided to get married and were thus wedded in June 1965.

Susan reported that she had once entertained the idea of marrying a black man; but things simply did not work out that way:

> Most of the black men that I was interested in were more or less educated and had a lot to offer; but unfortunately they were not interested in me. Most of the ones who wanted to date me were more or less uneducated—didn't have too much to offer; and I really didn't care for them too much.

While she was in the South and in college, she thought she had to find a black man to marry; "but I had difficulty finding a man I could communicate with. The black men I met wanted a relatively submissive wife. This is not the case with Ray."

Another black female respondent further pointed out that she had a problem with black guys because "I had so few

to choose from. I set out not to marry a man with less education than I.... I wanted a professional man. I knew that when
I went after the Ph.D., that closed a lot of doors."

Ironically, the black woman is further disadvantaged
when her traditionally greater education creates a gap between
her and the black man. While she may improve her social and
economic status, each year of school beyond the ninth grade
actually reduces her chances of finding a suitable black marriage partner. One black female states that: "The educated
black woman doesn't have anybody out there. Small wonder
why she views with rising concern the competition from white
women."[24]

Ostracized from Own Racial Group

One of the white brides who is presently in her second
black-white marriage says that once a white girl crosses the
color line, it is difficult for her to return to white society and
be accepted—especially if she has children. Before her first
marriage ended in divorce, she had one child. She attempted
to return home, but her family and friends would not accept
her black child. She even found it difficult to date white fel-
lows. Once they learned about her previous marital status and
the fact that she had a child, they no longer came around. She
stated that eventually she became a lonely individual, and
that the only alternative she had was to create some relationships with black people. She again started dating interracially
which resulted in marriage.

SUMMARY

Many unconventional social and psychological characteristics have been ascribed to individuals marrying interracially.
The present data do not support this argument. These findings strongly suggest that an overwhelming majority of the interracial dating and marriage on the part of these respondents
is not related either to some pathological abnormality or to
any crusade against prejudice. However, isolated cases involv-

ing "deviant" attitudes do exist.

Three of the black husbands' initial desire to date interracially unconsciously grew out of a vindictive feeling against the white male. In their opinion, seducing, dating, or marrying a white female is a breach of one of white society's most tabooed and sacred norms. Defiance of this norm serves as a source of psychological gratification. This is an indication of some of the frustrations and anxieties regarding social intercourse between members of the opposite sex and race.

There is fragmentary evidence that the so-called dominating personality of the black female possibly accounts for some black males seeking out white females as marital partners. Some blacks are of the opinion that white females are more affectionate, passive, understanding, and concerned about fulfilling the needs of their husbands. Data are too inclusive to categorically generalize about the alleged domineering attitude of the black female. In many instances, it is likely that her dominating actions are influenced by the low-socioeconomic status of her husband and its accompanying frustrations.

With a few exceptions, this group's motives for marriage do not appear to be any different from those individuals marrying in the conventional style (i.e., within one's own race). When male and female are involved in situations which are conducive for courtship, intimate relations might develop despite the race of the individuals involved.

5

Black-White Marital Combinations

MANY RESEARCH FINDINGS indicate that marriage between black males and white females occurs more frequently than it does between white males and black females. There is however a lack of consensus on this point as well as on the explanations for the difference. According to one report which is based on some 1960 census data, slightly more black females in the United States had white spouses than did black males; on the other hand, some 1967 data indicate that black men more often married white women.[1]

These data are inconsistent with nearly every research study reported. The difference may, in part, be explained by the lack of national data, central marriage records, and enforcement in reporting, as well as by the questionable nature of the data that are reported. The more general findings suggest that marriage between black men and white women are much more common than vice versa. Thus, there is much disagreement on this fundamental issue. There is also a lack of consensus on the reasons for a differential incidence of interracial marriage by sex.[2] This chapter examines black-white marital combinations and attempts to account for the sex patterns.

Hypergamous-Hypogamous Patterns

Robert K. Merton observed that intermarriage whether permitted or tabooed does not occur at random but according to more or less clearly describable patterns. Two of these patterns have received special attention. The first may be called *hypergamy*, a term which is adapted from its usage in connection with the Hindu caste system, wherein the female marries into a higher social stratum. The term *hypogamy* denotes the pattern wherein the female marries into a lower social stratum.

The Exchange Theory

Merton provides a logical explanation for the greater frequency of caste-hypogamy as compared to caste-hypergamy in the United States when he entertains the hypothesis that hypogamy is understandable in terms of the social structure. Two aspects of roles ascribed to males and females appear to be primarily relevant. These dimensions include socioeconomic status and access to the female population. For example, the latitude permitting women to seek an occupational career is not comparable to that accorded men. Occupational achievement is still considered the usual prerogative of the male, despite the larger participation of women in economic and public life. The male is "the provider," the chief source of economic status.[3]

Kingsley Davis sums up this viewpoint when he says that if marriages between black men and white women largely involved black males of high social status and white women of low social status, then the groom could trade his class advantage for the racial caste advantage of the bride. An exchange is in operation where the higher status black male offers his higher socioeconomic status for the preferred color-caste of the lower class female.[4] But given the current discriminatory and prejudicial aspects of American society, the economic-occupations penalty is great for the white male with a black wife. On the other hand, the black male with a white wife is penalized hardly at all, and he may even be helped by his wife's race.[5]

Accessibility to Females

The second difference in sex roles is contained in the prevalent code of sex morality. Despite some slight modifications, the female is more circumscribed in the range of allowable activity. It is commonly considered more appropriate that the male seeks out the female and initiates sex relations. For the most part, in the United States, black males have not had social access to white females. Moreover, social and sexual overtures from black males directed at white females have been strictly taboo.

The sex morality supports sex advances by the males; the caste morality more easily enables the dominant upper-caste member to initiate cross-caste sexual overtures. White males then may more readily initiate cross-caste sexual relations than either the white female, who lacks the male prerogative, or the black male, who lacks the upper-caste prerogative. This is the basis for most intercaste sex relations (not marriage) occurring between white men and black women.

Given the dominance of the white male with his relative immunity from active retaliation by the lower-caste male, there is no pressure to legitimize his liaison by marriage. Concubinage and transient sex relations are less burdensome and less damaging to his status, since these may be more easily kept secret and, even if discovered, are less subject to violent condemnation by fellow caste-members, since they do not imply equality of the sex partners.[6]

The difficulty with the "exchange theory" is that recent data have not shown any great discrepancy between the social status background of the white and black partners in an intermarriage. Current data indicate that there is an increasing tendency for these marriages to drift toward social, educational, and occupational homogamy. Research strongly suggests that Davis' accessibility hypothesis seems to be more useful today than that based upon economic penalties, though, of course, economic penalties may have been more applicable when first propounded.[7]

TRENDS IN MARITAL COMBINATIONS

Hypogamy (marriage between black males and white females) has been reported to exceed hypergamy (marriage between white males and black females) by ratios ranging from ten to one to four to one.[8] Louis F. Carter suggests that the preponderance of interracial hypogamy itself may be a myth, at least at the societal level.[9] An investigation, however, of a summary of empirical studies of the amount of black-white intermarriage from 1874 to 1965 for the country as a whole and nine states (Michigan, Rhode Island, Massachusetts, New York, California, Indiana, Hawaii, Nebraska, and Wisconsin) and for five cities (Boston, New York, Philadelphia, Washington, D.C., and Los Angeles), reveals a preponderance of *hypogamous* unions. Table 5-1 reports these findings.[10]

Prior to 1966, only one source contained data representing interracial marriages for the United States as a whole. From a 1939 national sample, Paul H. Jacobson reported 559 cases of hypogamy and 583 cases of hypergamy—roughly a ratio of one to one.[11] Carter contends that this finding, in direct conflict with the remaining published evidence, has received little comment. In an analysis of the Census Bureau's published one-in-one-thousand sample of the 1960 population, Carter found reports of thirty-three black-white marriages. Of these, seventeen were hypogamous, and sixteen, hypergamous.[12] Thus, his findings are consistent with those of Jacobson.[13]

The Hypergamous Tendency

The marital pattern that appears to be more pronounced for any given period depends upon how one looks at the data. When the data are analyzed on the basis of: *year husband first married* (i.e., when the husband was marrying for the first time), from before 1940 up to 1949, there were slightly more

Table 5-1
Summary of Empirical Studies of the Number of Black-White Intermarriages By Sex and Color of Marriage Partners, 1874-1965

Researcher	Area	Period	Number of black male-white female	Number of white male-black female	% Black-male-white female of all black-white marriages	% White-male-black female of all black-white marriages
Hoffman	Michigan	1874-1893	93	18	84	16
Hoffman	Rhode Island	1883-1893	51	7	88	12
Stone	Massachusetts[a]	1900	43	9	83	17
Stone	Boston	1900-1904	133	10	93	7
Stephenson	Boston	1900-1907	203	19	91	9
Drachsler	New York City	1908-1912	41	11	79	21
DePorte	New York State[b]	1919-1929	262	85	76	25
Wirth and Goldhamer	Boston	1914-1938	227	49	82	18
Wirth and Goldhamer	New York State[b]	1916-1937	424	145	75	26
Golden	Philadelphia	1922-1947	24	17	59	41
Lynn	Washington D.C.	1940-1947	19	7	73	27
Burma	Los Angeles	1948-1959	800	267	75	25
Barnett	California	1955-1959	921	252	78	22
Pavela	Indiana	1958-1959	72	19	69	31
U.S. Census	U.S.	1960	25,496	25,913	50	50
Heer	Michigan	1953-1963	862	267	76	24
Heer	Hawaii	1956-1964	59	15	80	20
Heer	Nebraska	1961-1964	6	2	75	25
Heer	Wisconsin	1964	38	5	88	12
Annella	Washington D.C.	1931-1965	523	295	62	38

[a]37 Towns and Cities [b]Exclusive of New York City

hypergamous marriages with an almost one to one ratio. But when we analyze it from the standpoint of: *when both partners were marrying for the first time,* from 1940 up to 1970 there is a greater tendency toward hypogamous unions. At this point, let us analyze the data from the first perspective. The census data of a bulletin on marital status based on a 5-percent sample with *year husband first married* show that up until 1949 there were more hypergamous (white male-black female) marriages. But from 1950 to 1960 this trend reversed itself—resulting in more hypogamous unions—but with an overall total, however, of 25,913 hypergamous, and 25,496 hypogamous unions for these decades. Here again, the national hypogamy-hypergamy ratio is roughly one to one but slightly inclined in the hypergamous direction. Table 5-2 describes these trends from before 1940 to 1960.[14]

Table 5-2
Black-White Marriages in the United States by Decade in Which Only the Husband Was Marrying for the First Time

Decade	Totals	Black male-white female	White male-black female
Before 1940	20,568	9,291	11,277
1940–1949	13,531	6,613	6,918
1950–1960	17,310	9,592	7,718
Totals	51,409	25,496	25,913

Source: U.S. Department of Commerce, Bureau of the Census, *United States Census of Population: 1960, Subject Report, Marital Status,* Report PC (2)–4E, pp. 160–161.

With respect to the *year the husband first married,* Carter is probably correct in saying that available samples cast some doubt on the representativeness of the largely few urban studies which have shown that interracial marriage in the United States is predominantly hypogamous. These marriages (before 1940 to 1960) in *which only the husbands were marrying for the first time* apparently suggest that these brides were not marrying for the first time. Moreover, these statistics reflect trends for over three decades rather than figures for only 1960 —which also show a marked reversal in the hypergamous pattern during the 1950-60 decade. Carter failed, however, to point this out. But the ratio still tends to be one to one.

The Hypogamous Tendency

When one looks at the data from the perspective of: *when both partners were marrying for the first time,* a different picture develops. For example, only during the 1940-49 decade were hypergamous unions greater. Even then the ratio was almost one to one. But since 1949, hypogamous marriages have been more prevalent. Table 5-3 reports these figures.[15]

Table 5-3
Black-White Marriages in the United States by Decade
in Which Both Partners Were Marrying for the First Time

Decade	Totals	Black male-white female	White male-black female
1940–1949	4,548	2,267	2,281
1950–1959	7,622	4,780	2,842
1960–1970*	23,771	16,419	7,352
Totals	35,941	23,466	12,475

*Again, the total number of mixed married couples in 1970 irrespective of the number of times married was 64,789, of which 41,223 consisted of black men and white women and 23,566 of white men and black women.
Source: U.S. Department of Commerce, Bureau of the Census, *United States Census of Population: 1970, Subject Report, Marital Status,* Report PC (2), pp. 262–263.

The national data from the Bureau of the Census on black-white marital combinations are inconsistent with data derived from empirical studies. For no periods in the history of this country has any empirical study reflected a preponderance of hypergamous marriages. By and large, they are extremely hypogamous. And only in 1960 did the census report a slightly greater hypergamous tendency (25,913 to 25,496) for the three previous decades.

If one views this phenomenon from both frameworks: *year husband first married* (and keeping in mind the findings of the empirical studies in urban areas from 1874-1965), and when *both partners were marrying for the first time,* the data strongly suggest that in the United States, there has been a greater tendency toward hypogamous unions between blacks and whites.

Throughout this investigation, I have advanced the idea that sexual relations between white men and black women, for the most part, have always been characterized by exploitation on the part of the white males. These associations infrequently eventuated into a legal marriage. What then accounts for the more pronounced hypogamous unions? An examination of the factors follows.

WHY HYPOGAMY?

Consistent with the findings of earlier empirical studies this investigation also reflects a hypogamous trend. This sample consists of thirty-three black male-white female and seven white-male-black female combinations. In Chapter 3, I discussed motives for interracial marriage. Some of the reasons given by some of the black male respondents might help explain why this pattern is more prevalent. These are: (1) white society being rebelled against, (2) the white female being a status symbol, and (3) the white female being less domineering. At the beginning of this chapter, I attempted to account for the hypergamous-hypogamous tendencies on the basis of the "exchange theory," and the idea of having access to the female populations. In addition to these explanations, three additional factors further lend support to the notion that the hypogamous marital pattern has always been more pronounced. These include: (1) the hypogamous nature of urban samples, (2) permanent availability of marriage partners, and (3) the role of "beauty" in the mate selection process. I will briefly examine each factor.

Urban Samples

Some states have never had laws forbidding interracial marriages. Even customs, attitudes, and sanctions in these localities were not as rigid toward those entering such alliances. But as indicated in Table 5-1, it is quite evident that in all of the states as well as a few of our large cities (for which we have data), black-white marriages have always included more black men and white women than white men and black women.

The greater amount of freedom exercised by black men in the mate selection process in these large urban areas contributes to an understanding of the hypogamous pattern. Despite the fact that white men had more latitude in choosing black marriage partners, it did not occur as often as compared with their black counterparts. According to Kingsley Davis,[16] since sexual relations have traditionally been relatively open between white males and black females in the United States, marriage has not been necessary between them in order for the male to legitimate such an interest. If, however, a black male is attracted to a white female, the stringency of the norms is such that he is more or less forced to legitimate that interest by marriage.

Based upon these urban samples and the fact that white men were allowed to perpetuate casual sexual relations with black women, it seems logical then that even if laws, customs, attitudes, and sanctions had been less stringent (toward black males) in many other regions of the country, this same pattern (hypogamous) would have prevailed. These conditions are coupled with another variable—i.e., the Western concept of beauty.

Cultural Standards of Beauty

On the basis of an exchange theory argument, the social advantages of hypergamy seem to exist primarily for the low status girl. For equity to occur, this type of exchange would require that the woman be exceptional in those qualities the culture defines as desirable. Depending on the society, qualities of women that determine status might include factors such as shade of skin color, facial and morphological features, and relative age. Typically, a woman is expected to use her attractiveness to gain certain legitimate ends such as recognition, status, and a husband.

Glenn H. Elder, Jr. suggests that throughout history, some women have been able to exchange their physical beauty for a young man's lineage, accomplishments, or mobility potential. American men rank physical attractiveness at or near the top among the qualities they desire in women, and this seems to be especially true of the upwardly mobile or strongly ambitious. Thus it would be expected that a male who achieves status through his occupation exchanges his social rank for the beauty and personal qualities of the female.[17]

In American society the dominant group naturally sets the norm by which feminine beauty is defined. Until recently, in many segments of our society, the more a female approximated those desired physical characteristics of the white female (as defined by society), the more she approximated the ideal of being beautiful. One would be hard put not to internalize at least some of society's notions of beauty—whatever the criteria might be. Black men just as white—or any man for that matter—to some extent are influenced by this cultural value.

Among the most clear-cut aspects of this process is the well-documented negative evaluation of skin pigmentation by blacks. Several decades of research have demonstrated that black themselves have defined dark skin as undesirable. Black periodicals have long contained advertisements for skin lighteners. All studies are consistent in finding that, in comparison with their blacker brothers, light-skinned blacks are preferred as marriage partners. This scale of values has formed the basis for judging the attractiveness of others as well as a determinant of self-esteem.

According to the nearly unanimous opinion of recent observers, however, the importance of skin color as a status determinant has been declining. As far as is known, no one has published any systematic evidence of this decline; and it has been recently concluded that marriage patterns by skin color have not changed recently.[18] In 1963, at a conference to study the Negro self-concept, black observers were suggesting that research on the influence of color on personality completed twenty or more years before "might be quite wrong in today's social context."[19] From many indications, importance of skin color is on the decline; but I would dare say that the syndrome has not completely faded away. I am suggesting that the notion of beauty in this country also accounts for a greater tendency toward hypogamous marriages.

Permanent Availability

Bernard Farber suggests a theory which also helps to understand the hypogamous nature of black-white marriages. The family, he says, should be regarded in terms of a lineage system or "orderly replacement" and the availability of individuals for marriage—"permanent availability." If orderly replacement is to occur, each family of orientation must provide for the continuance of its values and norms relating to patterns of family life and the socialization of children. Each family then serves to transmit cultural patterns.

In industrialized societies, lineage considerations in mate selection are at a minimum and kinship control over marriage dissipates. As a result, individuals become available for marriage with anyone at any time during their adulthood. Thus, in urbanized systems, a greater tendency probably exists for people to marry outside their particular cultural complex, and in some instances their racial context. This being the case naturally enlarges one's field of eligibles which are likely to include members of minority groups. Once these endogamous proscriptions are relaxed, unlike males of the dominant group who have always been permitted to make sexual advances toward minority group women, minority group males are now likely to initiate similar relationships with women of the dominant group—which more often are legitimated through marriage. Thus this contributes to the more widespread hypogamous pattern.

Intermarriage is on the increase not only because of a breakdown in parental control over mate selection but also because the traditional social categories which define intermarriage are themselves becoming vague and diffuse. As the various segments of the population lose their visibility, barriers to intermarriage are dissolved. In spite of the tendency for old categories to persist, other categories of mate selection such as personal characteristics will likely increase in relative importance.[20] These factors contribute even more to the hypogamous tendency.

Summary

Although research findings are inconsistent as to whether hypergamy or hypogamy is more widespread, the more general findings suggest that marriages between black men and white women are more prevalent. Two earlier explanations have been advanced for this striking pattern. One is the socioeconomic status of the black male. If these marriages involve black men of high and white women of low social status, an exchange is in operation in that the higher status black male offers his higher socioeconomic position for the preferred colorcaste of the lower-class white female. The second explanation is the accessibility hypothesis. Black men simply have not had social access to white women. And added to this, social and sexual overtures from black men directed at white women—for the most part—have been prohibited either by law or custom, or both.

In addition to this investigation, research conducted in the 1960s does not support the first explanation. The evidence suggests that, currently, individuals who contract a black-white marriage tend to be quite similar with respect to social, educational, and occupational characteristics. The accessibility hypothesis seems to be more effective in explaining the preponderance of black males (than does the exchange theory) because these men were more or less forced to have legitimate sexual liaisons with white women through marriage; this was not the case with white males in their relations with black females.

Even though the Bureau of the Census reported a slightly greater tendency toward hypergamous marriage for certain decades, in no period during the history of this country, have empirical investigations reflected this same trend. On the contrary, the studies indicate that for the urban areas researched a pronounced pattern of hypogamous marriage existed.

Some factors (as reported by the black male respondents) which facilitated the development of this hypogamous pattern are: (1) black men rebelling against white society, (2) black men's perception that the white woman is a status symbol, and (3) the idea that the white female is less domineering than her black counterpart. To these conditions, I have added three additional elements which also help to explain why this pattern is more widespread. These are: (1) the hypogamous nature of urban samples, (2) permanent availability (for marriage) of any person of age with any other individual irrespective of race, color, creed, or national origin, and (3) the role of beauty (as defined in Western cultures) in the mate selection process.

6

Dating, Weddings, and Marital Relations

ADJUSTMENT IN MIXED marriage is often difficult because of social disapproval and sometimes cultural differences. In entering such a union or even friendship, both the man and woman must violate the racial mores and meet the disapproval and perhaps ostracism of their friends. For an open courtship and married life, often the couple must be prepared to stand isolated from both the black and white communities.[1] This chapter investigates the dynamics of lifestyles and experiences of these forty families. First, it focuses attention on dating and wedding ceremonies. Second, it examines interpersonal relations between husbands and wives and parents and children. Third, the emotional and social development of the children is analyzed. Finally included is a discussion of the relationships between these couples and their families of orientation.

DATING

About thirty years ago, Drake and Cayton observed that the clandestine nature of most interracial sex relations in both the North and South indicated the strength of social controls over individual behavior. Nevertheless, there are scores of individuals on both sides of the color line who have no feelings of revulsion against such relations and who in varying degrees are attracted to one another. But if they were to maintain the approval of their associates, they could not be with a member of another race in a situation which carries sexual overtones.[2] Since that time, however, many social, economic, and political changes have occurred. It is now evident that many individuals are less concerned about what people think or say about them if they date or marry interracially.

It is explicit in this investigation and in the reports of the respondents that black-white dating is increasing and gaining more acceptance or toleration—at least in the Champaign-Urbana and Cambridge areas. The extent of this growth, however, is difficult to measure. Nevertheless, some attempt has been demonstrated. For example, a national poll conducted for *Life*[3] by Louis Harris and Associates indicates that almost one American in five has dated someone outside his or her own race. In the West and among young people age twenty-one to twenty-five across the nation, the figure rises to one in three. In the South it is less than one in ten.

Dating among these respondents most often took place in public (movies, clubs, on college campuses), in the homes of friends, or in the individuals' apartments. Initially, much of the dating was secret. A majority of the couples reported having difficulty concealing their relationship from parents and friends. With the exception of this element, this activity is no different from those dating within their own racial group. Parents' knowledge of their sons' or daughters' initial interracial dating is shown in Table 6-1.

Even though much of this dating was characterized by a clandestine beginning, two of the black females pointed out that they would have refused to become involved in a relationship if it had to be carried out in secrecy. One related her feelings:

> I would never have gone out with Richard.... Well, I used to hear these stories about whites who would never go out with blacks unless it was night. I don't know whether this was in the back of my mind or not, but I

Table 6–1
Parents' Knowledge of Their Sons'/Daughters'
Initial Interracial Dating

Respondents	Total	Number of parents knew	Number of parents did not know
Black males	33	13	20
White females	33	8	25
White males	7	3	4
Black females	7	0	7
Totals	80	24	56

would never have dated a white fellow if that's the way it was going to be. He would have to go out with me in the daylight—take me places. That's the way it would have to be. Otherwise, I don't want it—not sneaking around.

In general, these couples encountered no unusual or negative experiences during their dating and courtship stages. Several, however, mentioned receiving an unusual amount of stares. One of the brides stated that frequently, upon entering a public place, immediately she was conscious of everyone noticing that she and her black date were present. She asserts that:

Eventually we would soon blend in with the crowd and become less conspicuous. Some people have really gone out of their way to be nice and make us feel welcome. Once we went dancing, and this one guy came over to our table and kept telling us what great dancers we were. I think he was overreacting. He made it a point to be nice to us.

After dating for a short period, these couples became less concerned about the reactions of the larger community, friends, and eventually close relatives. They were strongly convinced that the choice to date or marry someone (irrespective of race, color, religion, or creed) is a personal matter; and this private concern and "inalienable right" should not be infringed upon by any religious or secular entity. If alleged friends strongly opposed their dating behavior, then there is some question as to if these persons were really friends. This same view was also expressed toward those parents and relatives who opposed interracial dating.

Most people—particularly the young, the affluent, and the better educated—have no quarrel with the trend of interracial dating—at least in theory. But when the questions begin to touch on the actual problems of interracial marriage, the responses take on an ambivalence that occasionally amounts to outright contradiction.[4] One of the white brides echoed this ambivalence: "My parents didn't care about me dating interracially; but now, marrying interracially, that's a different thing. They really didn't go for that."

Though many of these respondents' parents were unaware of their children's dating habits, the response to the Harris survey reveals an acceptance of the fact that black-white dating, like other contacts between the races, is increasing. When one of the white brides was asked: "Do you think many white women are now dating interracially?" She replied:

> We've gone down the street and seen many black and white couples; whereas, seven or eight years ago, this was a very rare thing. We're now finding out about each other. Some white girls are now more sympathetic to the black man. She cares enough to listen about what is going on. ...She will now dance with black fellows; talk with them and get to know them; and not think about what she originally thought.

Another white bride felt that some white women date black men because they are seeking diversion or something of the sort:

> I feel that the white girl is going out more with the black man because she's tired of the role of the establishment...that is, the middle-class white woman who has been mother and this sort of thing. She's sort of going for herself now. I think it's just a change. That's the whole thing. She's seeking different things now—a career—and an outlet from the establishment.

The response to the Harris survey reveals an acceptance of the fact that black-white dating, like other contacts between the races, is increasing.[5] The principle explaining this increase is that behavior becomes more prominent when there is greater opportunity and a more permissive attitude and when there is a smaller discrepancy between a person's values and his behavior. Those who do participate in interracial dating still have to pay the price of peer and community support.[6]

WEDDING CEREMONIES

Since interracial marriages are still far from being universally accepted, the majority of mixed couples prefer to have small, quiet ceremonies to which only a few close relatives and time-tested friends are invited. However, in sections of the country where there is less social chagrin about biracial alliances, such weddings are sometimes the biggest events of the season, take place in churches, attract crowds, and are reported in the daily newspapers.[7]

Nine of these couples had religious, but not highly publicized weddings. They were religious in that a minister officiated; and in few instances, the ceremony took place in a chapel. Of these ceremonies, whether religious or civil, the gatherings were small with only a few close relatives or friends attending. The number and type of wedding, and the number of relatives in attendance are shown in Tables 6-2 and 6-3.

Social pressures sometimes make it difficult for these weddings to be carried out conventionally—especially in a community which is still hostile or cold to mixed matrimony. Because curious people can seem so obnoxious, it is likely that these couples preferred to have small gatherings in an effort not to become targets of derogatory conversation. After repeating the nuptial vows, the couples next must make the proper adjustments required for a successful marriage. A discussion of this matter follows.

Table 6–2
Wedding Ceremonies

Weddings	Total	Marital Combination Black groom- white bride	White groom- black bride
Number of weddings	40	33	7
Civil ceremonies	22	18	4
Religious ceremonies	18	15	3

Table 6–3
Number of Respondents with Attendance at Their Wedding

Persons who attended	Race and Sex of Spouse Black grooms	White brides	White grooms	Black brides
Parents (both)	7	4	2	0
Parents (one)	3	2	0	0
Siblings	2	2	0	0
Other relatives Effective-kin*	6	6	2	0
Relatives Nominal-kin*	2	2	2	0
Close Friends	18	13	6	6

Effective-kin are those relatives who interact only occasionally—usually at ceremonial occasions such as weddings or funerals—but whose aid can be counted on in time of need. *Nominal-kin* are those relatives who are seldom seen and with whom no personal relationship exist. These definitions are taken from Bernard Farber's *Family: Organization and Interaction,* San Francisco: Chandler Publishing Company, 1964.

INTRAFAMILIAL RELATIONS

The fact that black-white marriages are rare is partially responsible for the limited amount of knowledge concerning these alliances. It is difficult to determine the success or failure of such marriages by the "criteria of divorce, desertion, and separation," as well as, by the welfare of the children. Much speculation has been based on little knowledge. Many statistics have been worked out by specialists to support the belief that black-white marriages lead to separation and divorce at a higher rate than do unmixed marriages. The truth is that the samples studied are far too small to allow for even an educated guess, let alone a significant prediction, of their possible success or failure.[8]

To compound the problem of predicting marital stability, at the time of the present study, most of the couples had been married less than five years. Therefore, attempts to assess marital stability would be speculative. Furthermore, it is difficult to measure the degree of happiness that exists among these couples. To get some notion of marital happiness, I relied on what the respondents themselves reported and to some extent on information obtained through informants.

In general the problems of black-white marriages apparently are no different from those of individuals who marry within their own racial groups. With respect to the degree of happiness that characterizes these families' interpersonal relationships the families are classified as follows: (1) normally happy families, (2) those with mild periodic strife because of black awareness, and (3) those with some gross incompatibility.

Normally Happy Families

A majority of the couples reported having developed a keen sense of awareness of each other's feelings because of differences in racial background. Since seven of the couples have been married an average of 13.4 years, this suggests that they have learned to live with those pressures confronting the intermarried. There were some problems but the respondents did not attribute race as the cause. In fact, their problems seemed common to all young marrieds. As time passed, many of these couples gained greater insight into the nature of some of their mild difficulties and became bent upon making their marriages work.

One black husband describes his special attempt to make his marriage stable:

> If we are going to make it, and deal with the ills of both black and white society, then we've really got to be strong together. We do not take each other for granted. Even though we are away from each other during working hours, before going to bed at night we discuss what has taken place during the day. If anything out of the ordinary happens, she calls me at work ... just to keep in touch.

This couple are convinced that had they married someone of their own race, many things would be taken for granted; and the acute awareness of the other's needs and feelings would not exist. By virtue of their being interracially married, the relationship is strengthened.

Impersonal association continues to be a characteristic element of the social life of many urbanites. Because of this impersonality, one couple reported being quite happy. The wife describes her feelings:

> We get along fine. We are quite happy. Nobody really bothers us, because we do not come in contact with very many people—except on our jobs. We work all week long. In fact, Dave works six days a week. When we get home from work, we are tired and want to get some rest. So, we just don't have time for too much socializing. We are happy the way we are.

This couple feels that their marriage is as happy and successful as any marriage could be. The husband explains that:

> When I first met her, I knew I loved her and I wanted her for my wife. I asked her to marry me and she finally did. And it is working out okay.

One couple married for twenty years pointed out that if they had not really loved each other and had not been able to live together without conflict, their marriage would never have survived. The husband explains:

> Man, we are the pioneers of interracial marriages. We married back in the days when things were really rough. Even in this town, relations between blacks and whites were bad. When we got married, this town was still totally segregated—I mean practically everything. Mixed couples today don't have to face half the problems we did...because this thing is becoming more accepted now. But we were in love so we got married. We have had our problems though...just like any other married couple. But I think we are about as happy as any other couple.

This couple presently lives in a comfortable home (which they are buying) in an all-black community. They have a sufficient income and appear to be happily married.

Two of the white brides who were previously married to white males have all-white children. They both reported being happy. The children accept their black stepfather just as any child would accept his own father. As one of the wives put it:

> We absolutely have no problem. The kids accept Ted as their father. In fact, they just love him. They don't know anything about their real father. We get along as one big happy family. Color has never been an issue with us. We just never think about that.

A majority of the families reported that quarrels or strife never include racial overtones. Quarrels are similar in nature to those of any married couple (i.e., over money matters, division of labor, disciplining children, and individual personality differences). The only time these individuals think of each other as being black or white is when some external force reminds them of it. There are, however, on the other hand, a few families who have experienced difficulties because of differences of racial backgrounds. Some of these are discussed in the next section.

Black Awareness and Intrafamilial Strife

External pressures often have intrafamilial effects. Although, two of the couples attribute some of the external pressure to black awareness; in some instances, it has served to unify the families. For those couples negatively affected by black nationalism, marital problems are confused with racial biases. One wife reported that some of her arguments are interpreted as racist:

> I never thought of his being black or my being white until recently. We have been more or less forced into this situation. I have been around blacks practically all of my life. And I always felt relaxed around them—but not anymore. Because they will let you know how they feel about you. This has really affected us. And it has also affected our marriage—even though we try to live with it.

The husband felt that larger society is to blame and that their happiness has certainly been affected because of black awareness.

Another black husband communicates a similar experience:

> The brothers and sisters often refer to me as a traitor to my race. I feel that black awareness is one thing, but the choice of a marriage partner is something altogether different. But those brothers who feel I have defected, I simply try to stay away from them. It doesn't bother me too much but it does affect my wife. And sometimes we have to talk about it. Things work themselves through.

Incompatibility and Family Strife

Four families had problems stemming not from black awareness but from incompatibility, excessive drinking by one white husband, and the unwillingness on the part of one black husband to get a job. When one of these couples first married, they "were very much in love," but gradually, the partners began to reflect dissimilar interest, values, and lifestyles. According to one of the wives:

> We thought the world revolved around each other. We were very happy. But as time passed, we simply couldn't get along anymore. Things really got bad. We couldn't discuss anything without getting in a heated argument. So we broke it off. It wasn't a racial thing. It was just that two

people who had nothing in common had made the mistake of getting married.

Another respondent felt that her marriage was strengthened primarily because it is interracial. The couple admired each other and never denied their race. Their arguments never had racial overtones; they both loathed prejudice. Although some people called them traitors, this had no effect on their interpersonal relationship. Their marriage "went on the rocks" not because of racial problems, however, but because of the husband's excessive drinking, which brought on violent behavior in the presence of the children. The wife's love changed to pity: "I was very hurt over our not being able to make it. Were it not for this drinking, we could have had a successful marriage." Moreover, she felt that marriage is a matter of love and understanding and that intermarriage serves as a common ground for the different racial groups to really get to know each other.

A third couple had several difficulties because of the husband's unwillingness to work. The white wife reported that as long as the husband was working, they got along well. It was the lack of income and other economic conveniences that created friction in their home and her relatives' unwillingness to accept these conditions. She commented: "It's not so much his being black that my kinfolk don't accept him. It's a matter of his not working. They feel that any man should work and support his family."

The intrafamilial problems of these families apparently are not different from those of conventional marriages: Although a few exceptions have been indicated, I wonder if they are in fact rare exceptions. Do these problems not exist for other couples of the same race?

Black-white marriages are often perceived to be conflict-ridden because this is thought to be a natural result of such marital unions. It is hoped that the reporting of some of the positive family experiences will provide a healthier climate for those who choose to enter such a marriage. The implications of this study might also ease the tensions and anxieties that are often said to be characteristic of the social life of children.

CHILDREN OF MIXED MARRIAGES

It is widely held that neither the black nor the white community accepts children born of mixed marriages. This is the most often repeated argument against intermarriage and is generally considered to be the most persuasive.[9] Gordon reports that these children are faced with problems which tend to produce within them reactions of guilt, insecurity, anxiety, and emotional instability.[10]

In spite of the problems commonly predicted for children, the majority of couples have children. Five are offspring of white-white parents and five of black-black parents by previous marriages. Approximately seventeen of the mulatto children can pass (at least in my opinion). A majority are too young to have developed a keen sense of race awareness or a self-concept. For example, of these seventy-two children, fifty-six are below age six. Although many questions were asked of the children, the information received is too fragmented and limited to lend itself to a concrete analysis of their self-images or society's reaction toward them. A few of the older children, however, did provide some insight into their relationship with larger society. Because of the difficulties in interviewing the children (such as some of the parents' unwillingness to permit them to be interviewed, limited social experiences, and a lack of understanding of some of the questions on the part of the offspring), I discuss their experiences, personalities, and social and emotional development with information mainly based on reports given by parents. Predictions as to what the future holds for these children are grounded in speculative statements made by the couples.

Emotional and Social Development of the Children

Twenty-nine of the children attend elementary and pre-schools. Their parents report that generally speaking they had made a normal adjustment. Occasionally, however, they have been confronted with racial matters. For example, one little girl came home from kindergarten and asked her mother why was she black, and expressed the desire to be some other color. The mother replied: "Your father is black and the situation cannot be changed."

In a similar vein, an informant reported that one offspring light enough to pass (who lives in a black community) returned from school one day and raised the question: "What am I? The white kids at school say I am Negro; and the Negro children in the neighborhood say I am white. Am I black or white?"

In talking with some of the children, I became aware that they are aware of different shades of skin color, but have not yet learned the full significance society attaches to such. Two families who share a common household have a total of six children—three of whom might well be identified as white. When one little girl (who can pass) was asked to identify the race of each member of the two families—based on skin color —she did so quite accurately. First, she identified herself with emphasis as being white. She further distinguished between the other family members as being either white or brown but never black: "I am white. He's white. She's brown; she's brown; and you (referring to me, the interviewer) are brown."

As in the above case, it is apparent that some of the intermarrieds prefer not to use the concept *black* to refer to their children. Another black wife stated she prefers to use *brown* rather than *black*:

> When my little girl asked me what color she is, I told her that she's creamy brown. Because that's what she is. She's not black. She's not white. She is creamy brown.

This couple, with three children—ages twenty-one months, three and a half years, and six years—have not had any special problem, and "do not anticipate any." They point out that their children are too young to conceptualize social reality in terms of black and white. Moreover, being of the Baha'i religious faith, this family feel they will always be accepted within this religious group; and pressures will therefore not arise which will force the children to identify as black or white. The Baha'is encourage intermarriage.

There are two families in which there are three all-white children (offspring of previous white-white marriage), who reside with black stepfathers. These couples reported that presently the children have no problems. Intrafamilial relationships are congenial; the children call and refer to their black stepfathers as "daddy." The couples feel they have a normal family life. They "do not want additional children because of the extra burden." It is difficult to ascertain if this is the real reason since there could be a combination of factors. The financial strain in addition to some skepticism about producing children in a mixed marriage might serve as a more valid explanation.

In many instances, children themselves set the tone as to what ties families might eventually establish within the neighborhood, and, ultimately, whether children will be accepted. Young children, who seem so naively open, sometimes serve as an initiating force in bringing together many adults when under ordinary circumstances they would not have come to know each other.[11] For example, one couple have a five-year-old son with whom the white neighbors did not want their children to play. But the mother reports: "The kids took over and soon they were having him over for lunch and parties."

Six couples expressed some degree of pessimism as to the social adjustment of their children. One mother stated:

> So far, they have had no problems of identity. They are whatever color they want to be—whenever they want to be. They feel they belong everywhere. They have many friends and get along very well in school. I am glad they are mixed; and I tell them they are of all races. I feel though as they grow older, they become cautious and defensive, and more hesitant to declare their heritage.

In addition to this pessimistic view, two white mothers feel that one of the worst consequences that can befall children of mixed marriages is rejection by the grandparents. These mothers assert that their children "have no place on this earth because they are not accepted by anyone." They charge the public school system with promoting prejudicial attitudes and behavior; and thus strongly question the whole idea of sending their children to such schools. This reaction may to some extent be emotional and biased—in the sense that it is unlikely that everyone hates their children simply because they are products of interracial marriages. It could be that the parents seek more acceptance from people who are unwilling to grant it. Furthermore, I would suspect that some of this alleged rejection is not necessarily based on race. As one of the black wives put it: "Many of the public stares that mixed couples and their children receive are not based on hostility, but sometimes instead on curiosity and admiration."

Attitudes of Childless Couples

In view of the problems children are expected to have, it is interesting that only seven of the couples are childless. One couple stated that if they had children, they certainly would inform them as to their identity but contend that interracially married parents should be open enough to accept the racial identification the children choose. The husband is aware that an offspring with a "white skin" who is racially black might have difficulties regarding personality development. Repeated frustrations, he claims, are not insurmountable. "With adequate guidance and emotional support, a child that finds himself in this type situation will eventually develop a sense of security and make a normal adjustment."

A second childless couple (ages, both thirty-two) have no plans for procreating. As the bride puts it:

> We really have no time for children. We want to finish our education. Furthermore we would have too much

explaining to do. We are concerned with the problem of overpopulation, but later on we might be willing to consider adopting children.

Perhaps this couple is reluctant to have children out of fear of creating additional hazards and problems for themselves. There is the possibility, in view of their ages, that they have tried but were unable to procreate. Why would they prefer to adopt rather than have children of their own? There might be some skepticism concerning their ability to deal with certain problems, and the feeling that they would be less affected if a biological bond did not exist. These explanations, of course, are conjectural.

A third couple, married for many years, have not been able to produce children. The husband expresses his attitude regarding children of mixed marriages:

> If we had children, we would tell them that, first, they are American, but would have to grow up as Negroes, because white people would not accept them. I do not foresee any problems a mulatto child might have that would be any different from those of a black child. Our children would identify themselves as Negroes. This, I would teach them.

Some of the other childless couples also gave financial reasons and a desire to complete their education for delaying having children. They have discussed among themselves some of the problems their children might have. However, they assume that when the children are old enough to really be affected by the reactions of society, things will have changed so drastically that many of the traditional problems will no longer exist.

Generally, a majority of the families are optimistic about the social and emotional development and adjustment of these children. They strongly feel that social, economic, and political changes will serve to gradually bring about a positive modification of many attitudes toward race in our society. This is not to say that some are not apprehensive about such matters.

The Status of Mulatto Children

Joseph R. Washington expresses an optimistic view regarding the status of an offspring of a black-white marriage. He observes that a child born of a black-white couple will be lighter than the black partner. Moreover, a light child has heretofore had a higher status in the black community because of the feeling that being "light" is nearest to approximating the skin color of the dominant group, and therefore has advantages which in most cases do not accrue to the darker child. Even this advantage, however, is waning in an age of the "instant Negro."[12] Moreover, the chances are also better for a light child to gain acceptance by white grandparents and relatives. Such a case is reported by one of the white mothers:

> When Rody was first born, he was very light. Grandmother, my uncle and aunt would always come over, and take him home for whole weekends. They just loved him. But as he got older, he grew a little darker. When this happened, they were not so ready to take him home. It seemed that their feelings changed. As long as he was real light, they didn't seem to mind. But the minute he started turning darker, they stopped keeping him. But every now and then, they will come by and take him home—but not like they used to.

Washington further notes that although he is lighter, the child is considered black in this society, and from the child's perspective there is no more difficulty in getting along with people than is experienced by a child of black-black parents. By the time the child enters college or is ready for work, the color of his skin might already be an advantage, which he may or may not wish to use. Thus, whether on the family, personal, or societal level, the child of a black-white marriage has all disadvantages of being black mitigated by some of the advantages of appearing light or white.[13]

Relations with Families of Orientation and Other Kinsmen

Humiliating experiences are not at all uncommon for the racially intermarried. A majority (26) of these marriages are not accepted by the white spouses' families of orientation (parents and siblings) and other close relatives. This is especially true for the brides. The black spouses' families, on the other hand, tend· to be a bit more receptive of such unions. This section discusses rejection and acceptance of these marriages by both black and white respondents' families of orientation and close kinsmen. A family of orientation is the family into which an individual is born.

Twenty-four of the thirty-three white brides' parents and relatives strongly opposed their marriage. Only two of the seven white grooms' intimate-kin expressed some reservations. Despite fourteen of these couples having been married from one and one-half to four years—and a few, even more—their parents and relatives have not changed their position or attitudes toward the marriage. Only nine of the thirty-three black grooms' parents initially expressed opposition; while two of the seven black brides encountered the same problem. A preponderance of the kinsmen of the black spouses however, gradually accepted the white partner. Table 6-4 presents the frequencies of rejection and acceptance.

Table 6–4
Rejection-Acceptance of the Respondents' Marriages by Families of Orientation and Other Kinsmen

Rejection-Acceptance	Totals	Marital Combinations	
		Black male- white female	White male- black female
Rejection by whites	26	24	2
Rejection by blacks	11	9	2
Acceptance by whites	14	9	5
Acceptance by blacks	29	24	5
Totals	80	66	14

ACCEPTANCE BY WHITE KINSMEN

Not all white spouses' parents and relatives oppose their marriage. There is often great opposition, but in a few cases, there is minor support. The kinsmen of three of the white brides disapproved of their marriage, but the families continue to maintain some contact. Six of the white brides reported receiving no opposition and thus extended family relations (in their opinion) appear to be normal. A brief discussion of three of these cases follows.

Susan and Ray

Ray and Susan (black female) were married in 1964. Both their families agreed to the marriage. The couple is of Baha'i faith. Susan's family has since also become Baha'is, while Ray's family is Presbyterian. Both have visited each other's families, and the marriage is completely accepted by all kinsmen. They maintain close ties throughout the kin network.

Edith and Chris

Edith reports that her parents and relatives completely accept her marriage. She once thought that they might have been a bit prejudiced; but after getting married, she learned that this was not the case at all. Her parents admire and respect her husband. Moreover, they simply adore their mulatto granddaughter. A similar attitude was manifested by the father of another white bride. When he was informed that his daughter was planning to marry interracially, his reply to the black groom to be was: "It's okay with me. But I would like you to know you're getting a spoiled brat. I'm happy for the both of you."

Brenda and Norman

Neither Brenda's father nor any of her relatives knew she was dating across racial lines. After marrying, she informed her father by telephone: "I've got some good news for you; I don't know how you'll take it, but I'd rather tell you the truth about it. I married a Negro." Brenda's parents are now deceased, her mother being so at the time of her marriage. She has one brother and an older sister. She stated that they totally accepted her marriage.

REJECTION BY WHITE KINSMEN

Because of their marriages, twenty-four of the white brides are extremely alienated from their parents and intimate kin. This appears to be the most traumatic aspect of some of these marriages. The wives can accept most of the pressures generated by larger society, but for them and their children to be rejected by their parents seems to be devastating. It is difficult for these women to understand how supposedly loving parents can let such a thing as marriage to a black person disrupt such a "sacred bond" as between parents and child.

All twenty-four brides reported interesting negative experiences with their parents and close relatives. Since their encounters are too numerous to include, three cases which appear to be representative of these spouses' relationship with close relatives have been selected as illustrations. These include Margie and Boyd, Jenny and Jerry, and Hilda and Lennie.

Margie and Boyd

Margie and Boyd dated five years without her parents ever knowing anything about the courtship. After the two decided to marry, Margie felt that it was best she let her parents know. She describes what happened:

> Their reaction was disastrous. My mother nearly went crazy and father cried. Since his "cryings" really affected me, I promised him I would wait until my twenty-first birthday. They even offered to buy me things and send me to Israel if I didn't marry this man.

Margie has had no contact with her parents within the past five years. They consider her as dead. However, she has kept in touch with her brother, who she says "understands the situation." She reports that the loss of contact with her family used to upset her, but now she accepts the fact and no longer worries about it.

Jenny and Jerry

Jerry and Jenny met while they were students and were married in May 1969. She has not seen her parents since the week prior to the wedding. She writes to them but they never answer. She keeps in touch indirectly through her uncle and cousins. She depicts her relationship with her parents:

> I had told them everything about Jerry except that he was black. They thought he was just fantastic. Then I decided I wanted them to meet him. "I think you ought to know ... he's black." That's when they blew the whistle. Things got very bad—very tense to say the least. My parents were very much against the marriage; so they refused to meet Jerry. They sent me to a psychiatrist. They also hired a detective to watch me—to make sure I didn't see Jerry—which really didn't work because I kept up my same habits ... seeing and dating him. I saw the psychiatrist for seven months. I was very confused because I was torn between the love I felt for my family and the love I felt for Jerry. I was running around ... didn't recognize people I knew. I didn't talk in complete sentences. I was having a rough time. So this psychiatrist really helped me in a number of ways.
>
> My parents contacted my sister in California and had her come live with me to make sure I didn't elope. One day Jerry and my sister spent seven hours talking; and the only thing that came out of that lengthy conversation was she thought Jerry was a fantastic guy. There wasn't anything wrong with him or me; but the situation itself was morally wrong. So, she told me that if we got married, she would have absolutely nothing to do with me; and would never acknowledge me as a sister; and if she got married, she would never want her children to meet mine.

Because of the behavior and attitudes of Jenny's parents and sister, she went on what she called a "suicidal trip." She became exceedingly nervous, could not sleep at night, and thought she was developing stomach ulcers. At the time, she was living on the sixteenth floor of her building. On several occasions, she had given serious thought to destroying herself by jumping out of the window. She awoke one morning unable to talk. Her roommate called the infirmary; a doctor came over and she was finally admitted to the hospital. She then talked to a psychiatrist for about four hours without making a complete sentence. She recalls:

> I couldn't say anything; nothing would come out. I was in a cold sweat. I was trying to get my thoughts out of me. I couldn't finish a sentence because my thoughts were changing so fast. He told me that he understood the basic ideas I was trying to verbalize; and that I was a very bad candidate for suicide—that I shouldn't consider that anymore because I wouldn't be able to do it. I liked life too much for that. He said if it were possible, I should not see my family nor Jerry for a while—to just stay alone and try to work things out on my own—which was something I wanted to do. I had a vacation coming up anyway.
>
> Nevertheless, I did visit my family, but the relationship was extremely strained. My parents did not trust me anymore or believe anything I said. They interrogated me about my activities, including whether or not I was still seeing Jerry.
>
> Upon my return to school, I had another visit with the psychiatrist. I had then made a decision as to what I wanted to do. In order to keep peace, I was going to continue to see Jerry and lie to my parents about it. The psychiatrist agreed that if I felt comfortable about it, that was the best thing to do at the time. I truly felt that I had made the right decision. So after that, things got progressively better.

In an effort to cope with her dilemma Jenny continued her sessions with the psychiatrist. Jenny's parents interpreted her wanting to marry a black man as a manifestation of a much deeper psychological problem. The therapy with the psychiatrist began with a discussion of her early childhood, her relationship with her father, mother, and sisters. Attempts were made to determine what type of experiences she had internalized that facilitated her developing certain values and interests that might be related to her desiring to marry someone black.

In many instances, this data suggests that it is not at all uncommon for the white respondents' parents to feel that something is psychologically wrong with a white person who is motivated to marry someone who is black. The following case of Hilda and Lennie further corroborates this point.

Hilda and Lennie

Lennie and I attended the same high school. We had been friends for a long time. We liked each other, so we started dating. When my mother found out about it, she became upset and tried to stop it. But I kept on seeing him. She then sent me to the Probate Judge. When my family told the judge about me dating a black man, he said: "Oh my gosh, a nigger"—and that's all he said. At that time, I was fifteen and they thought I shouldn't run around with blacks because that wasn't right. The judge didn't actually talk with me but to my mom, and she told me he said that I should be sent to the state hospital because I was having problems with my family; and if I didn't want to go voluntarily, he would probate me. Then that would be on my record. So I volunteered because I didn't want it on my record. I went out there and we had group therapy. They made you talk to everybody.

This one doctor said I shouldn't be out there, and after twenty-three days, he tried to get me out but the judge said I had to stay thirty days, so I stayed thirty. But then he wanted me to promise that I wouldn't associate with any black people before I could leave. But I didn't make that promise. Then he (the judge) made me stay sixty days. But, I still didn't make that promise. Then he made me stay ninety days. But I could leave if I promised not to associate with any black people. At first I was strongheaded; but then I knew they wouldn't let me out unless I said it; so I made the promise.

I didn't have no medicine or *nothing*. I was in the unit with the people who took drugs and we just sat around and talked. We would draw for art therapy. The bill was 4,000 and some dollars and my mom sent it right to the judge. I don't know who paid it.

As soon as Hilda was released from the hospital, she started doing exactly what she promised she would not do. This couple now has a child and they appear to be relatively happy with each other.

A majority of these wives do not accept the idea of their parents and other close relatives rejecting them forever. They view this behavior as an immediate reaction to an unconventional act. As one bride puts it: "Eventually they will have a change of heart and look at things in a different light."

A second bride further emphasized this point:

> My other sister feels that I am an enigma to the family. My father and mother are generally hurt about the whole thing; and aren't about to communicate with me. I feel that with time, or if something would ever happen to me— it would have to be one of those situations—that would bring us together again. And they would finally meet Dempsey.

Rejection by Black Kinsmen

Until recently a few of the interracially married blacks' relatives and some segments of the black communities manifested mild reluctance toward accepting mixed marriages (at least in the early stages) , but gradually, the white spouses became integrated into their husbands' families and ultimately made their adjustment in black communities. However, with the advent of "black awareness," eleven of these families have felt the backlash of black communities.

For example, Crane's family does not accept his marriage. When he told his mother that he was going to marry a white girl, the reply was: "You are going to have the worst time in your life, because society is not set up for mixed marriages." Crane's family continues to accept him, but not his spouse or his marriage. Moreover, his older sister told his wife, that "we will never accept you because you are white."

One of the white brides reported that once they were accepted by her black in-laws but now that is no longer true. She asserts:

I'm told that I can't bring my children home to see their white grandmother. This hurts—not for me but my children. Not only are they not accepted by the white grandparents, they are not accepted anymore by the black grandparents. The Negro grandparents don't want to be bothered with them anymore because they are now too involved in the black movement. Black people are rejecting us now as much as whites. We have nobody but ourselves. We don't know anyone we can really call on. We sometimes seek out other mixed couples for friends.

SUMMARY

The trend in interracial dating apparently is not only on the increase, but the secretiveness previously associated with it is also declining. This increase and change in attitude may in part stem from the general changes in public interracial interaction. As was the case in the past, however, a majority of the weddings in the present investigation continued to be performed with little publicity, with a small number of persons in attendance.

A preponderance of the families reported being relatively happy. As far as marital problems are concerned, theirs are no different from those of any other marriage. Quarrels or other family disagreements seldom carry racial overtones.

Most of the parents feel their children will not encounter insurmountable discriminatory problems. They attribute this to the changing nature of race relations in American society. They say that "things are getting better," and that future America will become increasingly free of racial prejudices. A few families, however, do not concur in this opinion.

Humiliating experiences are not at all uncommon for some of the racially intermarried. Many of the respondents' kinsmen oppose these marriages. Despite some couples having been married for several years, most of the white parents and relatives have changed neither their negative position nor their attitudes. On the other hand, the kinsmen of a majority of the black spouses are more receptive to mixed marriages.

The extent to which negative feelings are increasing in the black communities is uncertain. It appears that black communities are divided on the issue of interracial marriage. Some blacks view this phenomenon as one channel through which equality can be achieved. Others feel that at this point, for a black to marry across the "color line" is inconsistent with a developing sense of a black peoplehood. Likely the general atmosphere is one of acceptance by a majority in black communities, toleration by others, and total rejection by a minority.

7

Relations with the Larger Community

INTERRACIAL MISCEGENATION AND marriage have long been socially and, at one time in some states, legally prohibited. Those who selected a partner outside their race did so in the face of possible fury from all levels of society, beginning with family and friends and extending to the community at large. Yet race and religion as criteria of eligibility have been affected by the general change in values, especially among the young. Despite the fact interracial marriages are on the increase, there is still a lag in attitudes between young people and adults. And thus, vestiges of racial jealousy and fear are exhibited by both black and white adults.[1]

This chapter describes the (1) positive, (2) neutral, and (3) negative reactions from friends and neighbors in both the black and white community. There is a discussion of the families' relations and experiences with casual encounters—i.e., people in stores and on the streets. Some attention is also given to these couples' experiences with many of our social institutions which are controlled by whites. These include: (1) schools, (2) hospitals, (3) law enforcement agencies, (4) housing, and (5) employment. As there is no attempt to describe statements from each family regarding its relationships with the larger community, only those cases are included which are felt to be representative of the different kinds of reactions generated by larger society.

Even though a majority of these couples encountered extreme opposition because of their marriage, eight families reported having congenial relationships with the white community—especially neighbors and friends (those individuals who were close associates of the couple before their marriage). Twelve of these couples reported having no difficulties (including friends and neighbors). Twenty of the families related being ostracized and feeling completely rejected by the white community—including friends and neighbors. Fourteen families experienced positive reactions with the black community; sixteen, neutral; and ten, negative. The degree to which these families are accepted/rejected by the black and white community are shown in Table 7-1.

Table 7–1
Reactions of Community Toward Black-White Couples

Community and Nature of Relationships	Total Number of Couples	Marriage Combination	
		Black male-white female	White male-black female
White Community			
Positive	8	2	6
Neutral	12	12	0
Negative	20	18	2
Black Community			
Positive	14	14	0
Neutral	16	8	8
Negative	10	10	0

RELATIONS WITH THE WHITE COMMUNITY

This investigation shows that attitudes of the white community toward black-white marriages vary from complete acceptance to a seemingly apathetic state to that of total outright opposition. Some of the respondents, for various reasons have not yet been involved in situations with (their white neighbors) that lend themselves to an evaluation of the exact extent to which they are accepted or rejected.

Positive Reactions

One of the black grooms who is a teacher-musician indicated being completely accepted in the white community in which he and his wife live. They both have a wide circle of white friends. They attend parties, picnics, and many other social functions. Visits in each other's homes are quite frequent. The husband observed:

> If the people around here are prejudiced, I haven't detected it. They have always treated me in a friendly manner. We get along quite well. If they have prejudice feelings, they do a good job of hiding it. Then maybe this is due to the nature of this community. These people are middle class with open minds.

An interesting feature about black-white marriages is that the white male/black female marital combination appears to be less repulsive to many whites than that of the reverse pair. Five of the white male/black female couples live in predominantly white neighborhoods. They reported having no trouble whatsoever. According to one of the husbands:

> We have been living in this building for three years. We know most of the people in the immediate area; and most of them know us. They seem to accept our marriage. They treat us okay. In fact, I have never observed any signs of unfriendliness.

Another of these couples (white male-black female) who have three children reported having similar experiences. Their neighbors are quite friendly. All the children play together. When parties are given, all the kids are invited. The husband points out, however, that he is aware that many people are opposed to mixed marriages; and therefore, they have always tried to live in a community in which few racial problems were anticipated.

There are several explanations for the seemingly greater acceptance of this marital combination. First, the generally higher socioeconomic status of the white male makes it much easier for him to acquire housing in those residential areas which might be relatively free of overt racial bigotry. Secondly, two of the communities in which these couples reside are adjacent to a university which might suggest certain social characteristics of the residents. Thirdly, it might be that the black female is less repulsive to society when she violates the marital rules of racial endogamy. Finally, evidence suggest that this is an indication of an increasing acceptance or greater toleration of mixed marriages by certain segments of the population. There is no intent to convey the idea that these same families would find all communities equally accepting.

Neutral Reactions

Twelve of the black male-white female couples pointed out that they have not experienced obvious rejection or overt acceptance by white society. They expressed the general view that "we keep pretty much to ourselves." One of the husbands further commented:

> It's pretty hard to tell if we are accepted or rejected. We have lived in this neighborhood for one and one-half years. The neighbors speak to us . . . we speak to them. They don't attempt to help us in any way, nor do they try to harm us.

Although a second couple see and speak to their neighbors, they have little contact with them. The wife feels that maybe "one is waiting for the other to initiate conversation." A third family is uncertain as to how their white neighbors feel about them. This couple is seldom home. They spend a considerable amount of time on their jobs and attending night classes for college credit. They haven't had any repercussions. It is difficult to determine, if given the proper conditions, just how these families would be received. It is my guess that since nobody has made their stay uncomfortable, an attitude of apathy probably defines the mood of their neighbors.

Negative Reactions

Although several of the couples have had either positive or neutral experiences, at least twenty of the families reported having received negative reactions. For example, one of the black husbands feels that if one is black he cannot separate himself from the black community; and points out: "Wherever we go, we are the black community." This couple cannot rest assured that what happens to the "brothers" and "sisters" in the ghetto will not happen to them in the white community. They feel that no matter where or when blacks move into a neighborhood, the residents think the neighborhood will begin to deteriorate and eventually become another ghetto. According to the husband:

> When we move into a white neighborhood, we are put through a test. We are watched to see if we are keeping our house clean and the yard tidy. If we pass the test, the neighbors might deliver a couple of "hellos."

The wife stated that at times some of their white neighbors and acquaintances will associate with them. But these, she explains, are hypocrites. She expresses the hostility she has developed:

> They will talk, smile, and laugh while in your house, but when they are out with the rest of the white world, they don't want to associate with you. They are not ready to accept us in their world. You can mistreat a dog; and if you keep on mistreating this dog, he's going to turn on you. In a way you might say that's what's happening to us. We are actually tired. We want to walk down the street and say: Look at us! We are happy going out together. But we can't do that. All the time we are ready to fight. Why should we have to feel like that when we go out? Why do I have to live like a wreck? And to a point, I am a wreck. We have lived in this house for about six months...

> and absolutely nobody has come to the door and said:
> hello, we would like to meet you. In the first place, this
> house is out in the sticks; and nobody . . . absolutely nobody
> from around here will even associate with us . . . not even
> with the kids.

This couple feels, however, that there is a small percentage of white Americans who are not prejudiced and will work enthusiastically to bring about change. Several of the other families have encountered similar experiences.

REACTIONS FROM CASUAL CONTACTS

Several of the couples reported receiving stares from passersby while shopping or simply being in public together. Some of the respondents interpreted these stares as hostile reactions, while others construed them as signs of curiosity and admiration. Two of the couples reported that because of the stares, as much as possible, they deliberately refrained from being in public together.

At the time of the interview, two families were sharing a common household in a predominantly white community. They had sought out each other because of a need to interact with friends in a similar situation. The wives, especially, lived a lonely and isolated life. They had little contact with either the black or the white community. One of the brides describes some of her problems.

> I have no life in this country because my children are
> not accepted and they are uncertain as to their identity. My
> kids are rejected by black and white children. Whites think
> my kids are black; and the blacks think they (the children)
> are white. Blacks started treating us this way within the
> last two or three years.
> It's hurting to see people spit in the street at your
> children. People will stand and absolutely . . . the saliva will
> practically run out their mouths—gawking at you and your
> children. Some white folks are animals you know. The two
> of us can go shopping . . . myself and Clara . . . we're just
> two people . . . that is two white people; then we can go
> shopping together with our children, and we are suddenly

monsters . . . just plain dirt. You get tired of people hating you so much. We live on our own. We have just us, and we get tired of that. Sometimes I feel as if I hate 90 percent of white Americans . . . because of the way they have treated me and my children. But I really don't hate anybody; it is difficult for me to understand how some people can be so cruel simply because one is interracially married.

I find that a lot of the poorer class whites are the ones who hate and really make it bad for you. The more educated ones may have themselves together a little more. They may not really be that way inside, but it comes out maybe differently because of their positions. But the ones who are not educated are the poorer class whites; and it is nothing for them to spit on us. They feel that we are down on their level and that we are pulling their level down even more. And the same ones that spit on me couldn't make me a hot cup of tea if I were dying.

Some of these poor whites will push you around—just take over. One day, we took the kids out to the fair to ride on Santa's train. We had been standing there a good fifteen minutes in the cold rain—waiting for the train. All of a sudden the train pulls up, and a whole bunch of other kids and their mothers came along . . . and you could call these ladies honkies—because our kids were there first; but they wanted their children to ride first. We got our kids on that train! And this one lady told us off; they will just take over—treat you like dirt.

Unlike the above couple, some of the respondents reported noticing no unusual stares or reactions. Moreover, when they are in public places (together), some people even "go out of their way to be nice to them." It appears that specific places, circumstances, and the individuals themselves often determine how these couples are treated by the larger community.

EXPERIENCES WITH THE CHURCH

Only six of these families are actively affiliated with the church. After marriage, the couples tended to sever ties with their congregations. It is unknown as to what extent their marriages deterred church attendance. Moreover, it is difficult to determine the degree to which they would have been accepted had they continued active membership. One couple and their three children, however, who are of Baha'i faith, reported being totally accepted in their church. The Baha'is encourage racial interaction of all sorts. Generally, most of those who attend church regularly have had no problems. On the other hand, one couple reported having unpleasant experiences with the Catholic Church. The husband commented:

> Ministers are supposed to be enlightened as far as social ills go. But some of these same ministers are the prostitutes of the church. Every couple has their own crisis period. But when we are having ours, I found that the same church officials who are against divorce will turn around and recommend that we separate. What they are really saying is that you should divorce... not because you are man and wife, but because you are black and white.
>
> There are people who are supposed to be religious and some of these same individuals will come to you and say: "If I had a son or a daughter that married a black, I would have killed them." When we attend church, we might enter after the sermon has begun, but as far as the congregation is concerned, the sermon stops. We become the sermon. Finally, we got tired of this, and just quit going. This didn't only happen here; it happened everywhere we have lived. We got out of the church because of this. But, later we realized that this was wrong. We were taking our aggression out on the church for the human beings in it. We shouldn't feel that every Catholic Church, priest, or nun is like this. But many Catholics do condone racism.

This couple decided to stop attending church because of the racial prejudice and discrimination to which they were subjected. Not only has a majority discontinued going to church, the families hold membership in few other organizations. They feel there is little to gain by joining associations.

HOSPITALS

In the process of obtaining medical services, thirty-nine couples reported having experienced no difficulties. When it was necessary for the children to receive medical care, the mothers and fathers detected little, if any, racial prejudice or discrimination from hospitals and their personnel. The same is true of situations in which only a white mother might accompany her child to doctors' offices or to hospitals, or a case when a black husband might escort his wife. Only in one instance (when one of the brides went to the hospital for child delivery) did a couple report receiving unfair treatment from a hospital. One of the nurses decided to express her views toward mixed marriages. The wife related the incident:

> I had just had a baby twenty minutes previous. I wasn't feeling good. You know how one feels when she has just given birth to a baby. This nurse came up to me and asked: "What makes you tick anyway?" I was so tired, I just looked at her. And I finally said: "What did you say?" She said: "Well, what makes you tick? What a disgusting way to be married! That black man is your husband!" And I said: "I never looked at it like that before. I guess that black man is my husband." She then told me that if I were her daughter she would have killed me...that I would never have lived...especially to have a baby. She went on to say that she had lived with black people and just knew they were not to be mixed with white people. And therefore, I was the lowest dirt she had seen come by her as a nurse.

One of the nuns who was assigned to the ward, simply to visit and talk with patients to see if they were having problems, failed to visit this respondent—although she made regular visits to the other patients. The husband interpreted this as an act of racial discrimination and reported it to the hospital officials.

This mother also remembered other humiliating experiences. During a hospital visit, a nurse approached her and said: "Oh, foster baby?" The mother said "No." Then the nurse said: "Oh, you adopted her?" Again, the mother said "No." The nurse then said: "Well she doesn't look like you." The mother replied:

> Has it ever occurred to you people that she might look

like her daddy? Well, I'm sorry. Just because she got some
fuzzy hair on her head, you think she can't be mine. I laid
and had her just like you laid and had yours. I suffered
the same pain.

Several interns asked if she were married to someone Spanish or Mexican. She said they would never ask if she were married to a black. In general, with the exception of this case,
these families relationships with hospitals and medical personnel have been cordial.

THE POLICE

Two of the couples have been harassed by local policemen. A few others reported hearing rumors about the police
"being out to get them." One black groom stated that before
he got married, he occasionally would go "joy riding" with
some white female friends—which often resulted in immediate
encounter with the police. He describes what frequently
happens:

> Sometimes, these girls would ask me to go on errands
> ... I'm kind of hesitant at times because I don't like to be
> riding around with them. They seem like a magnet because
> they are riding with me. If you are a black man, you can
> be driving along, not violating any traffic laws, and be
> stopped and harassed because a white woman is in the car;
> whereas, otherwise they probably wouldn't even notice you.

A second black groom feels that he has been subjected to
police harassment primarily because of his marriage:

> One night, on University Avenue, me and my old lady
> was rapping; the man came up and said I was disturbing
> the peace. He hooked the handcuffs on me ... put me in
> jail for three days ... because these white police don't want
> to see no nigger with a white woman.

The wife further stated:

> I think that's wrong. When he was married to a black
> woman, they fought all the time ... the police have arrived
> on the scene and didn't say anything. But black and white

policemen alike will try to get a white girl on a prostitu-
tion charge if they even see her with a black man. They
think that he is a pimp or she hustles for him.

A second wife reported an incident with the police:

> I was still asleep, I heard a banging at the front and
> then at the back door. I went to the front door and some
> policemen were there. There were also some at the back
> door. I answered the front door and asked: "What's going
> on here?" One policeman said: "We are looking for a girl . . .
> Judy Mink." I told them I didn't know anyone by that
> name. I then asked: "Why did you come here?" They said:
> "Well, somebody told us all the names of the mixed
> marrieds around here and this girl's white; and she's going
> with a Negro. She's wanted for forgery."
>
> I told them I didn't associate with white trash. Then
> one said: "What makes you think she's white trash?" Well,
> if you want her for forgery, she must be white trash. I
> asked them if they wanted to come in and look for them-
> selves. They didn't because they didn't have a search war-
> rant. I called my husband on his job. He in turn called
> the police station who said these officers would come out
> and apologize. They didn't come; so I called the Head
> Officer. He came out and apologized. Meantime, I showed
> him our marriage license to prove we weren't shacking up.

These couples are more or less convinced that their marriage generated this harassment. For to date or marry interracially was strictly a breach of the norms. Moreover, possibly
the policemen felt that "these white women might have been
engaging in deviant or illegitimate activities inasmuch as they
were involved with black men."

HOUSING

An earlier investigation reveals that one mixed couple
(white female) living in a luxurious Manhattan apartment
reported being constantly harassed by mysterious calls in the
middle of the night. They had suffered many torments. Police
had pestered them; strangers had threatened them; and friends
had snubbed them. From time to time, their mailbox was

stuffed with unprintable letters; their automobile tires were repeatedly slashed; their rest was interrupted night after night. Wearying of it all, ultimately they decided to move into a Harlem hotel where many mixed couples had found sanctuary.[2]

Hearing this story, *Ebony* became interested and wanted to find out if this situation were typical of the interracially married. Editors and correspondents interviewed black-white families from New York to California. They discovered that the residential pattern was never the same. In Los Angeles, mixed couples live in virtually every part of the city. In Chicago, they spearheaded the population movement that brought blacks into exclusive Hyde Park for the first time. In Washington, D.C., they settled in black communities. In New York, they resided for years in Harlem and St. Albans, Long Island; yet many were also found in the white communities.[3]

In areas where interracial marriage is viewed without too much hostility, mixed couples may be found in almost all types of neighborhoods.[4] This is the situation that characterized the Champaign-Urbana couples. For example, of those who were contacted for interviews, nine of the families lived in either all black communities or in border or transitional areas; three in a mixed neighborhood; and the majority (nineteen families) were dispersed throughout the larger white community. Of the Cambridge, Ohio, couples, only one family resided in a predominantly white community; the others in either all black or relatively mixed neighborhoods. In Birmingham, Alabama, and Jackson, Mississippi, they all live in black neighborhoods. The sex of the white partner seems to determine where the couple will live. If the husband is white, the couple will ordinarily live in a white neighborhood. If he is black, the reverse is usually true. A black photographer in New York, married to a white stenographer, explained that "the problems of survival in white areas become too great for the black male partner. When a black man marries a white woman, she comes to him. He doesn't go to her."[5]

In a similar vein one of the white wives in the present investigation commented that:

> When the white female crosses the line—especially in marriage—she usually tends to follow the ways of her husband. So, therefore, when a white woman picks a black man, she automatically follows most of his ways. She identifies with him instead of going back to her culture.

Interestingly enough, the housing dilemma faced by interracial pairs appears to be less severe if the wife is black. One explanation may be that the economic status of the average white male in America is higher than that of his black counterpart. In any case, these couples seem to have greater freedom in choosing their homes. Some have never lived in black communities.[6]

One of the black husbands reported that the problems of a white male/black female marriage are much milder in comparison to those of the black male/white female. Of the six white male/black female couples who were contacted for interviews, five have always lived in predominantly white communities. The white husbands experienced little difficulty in getting suitable housing. Moreover, they have had few problems with their neighbors.

In attempts to obtain housing, many of the families had problems. On the other hand, a few had no difficulties whatsoever. But in order to move into the neighborhoods of their choice, numerous mixed couples have had to resort to deception. When the agent or owner is known to be white, the white spouse makes the contact and negotiates for it. If he is black, then the black partner handles the arrangements.[7]

One black husband related that he sent his wife to a real estate agency to make an application for an apartment. Thus, she made a $50 deposit and was given a receipt. Upon approval of the application, both of them appeared at the office to pick up the key. The manager said there was no record of an apartment being rented in their name. After presenting their receipt and explaining that their lawyer would investigate this matter, the company then acknowledged the transaction. However, after going through such a humiliating and dehumanizing experience, they decided against renting the apartment.

In an attempt to circumvent discriminatory practices in renting apartments, the wife describes the strategies they have used since the above incident:

> After that experience, whenever we saw a place we thought we liked, I would make an inspection to see if we really wanted it. If so, I would go get the place myself and we would move in. I didn't care what they would say or think. Because if you told them you were interracially married they wouldn't rent it to you anyway.

She further contrasted the difficulties of securing an apartment with those of renting a house.

> Although, at times, we had trouble, we could get an apartment much easier than we could a house. A lot of apartments are owned by large companies with the headquarters out of town. And these companies have contracts that say you can rent to a student, family, or anybody . . . it don't matter. But with houses, many are privately owned. In fact, the lady that owns this house we are living in now is English. It turns out to be that she isn't a prejudiced person. She has feelings like my own. We gave her references from where we had rented before; and when she was having them verified, they told her: "Do you know that her husband is black? Well, we want you to know." She told me about it. She said: "Your husband is black . . . you know they told me." She didn't ask me, so I didn't tell her. I used to be fool enough to do stuff like that but not anymore. I feel that if we could pay our rent, that's good enough.

A second couple stated that about three years ago, they contacted a female landlord who was listed on the university housing list, which by law meant she was supposed to rent to any person regardless of race, religion, or national origin. After an unsuccessful venture in trying to rent from her, they later learned that this woman discriminated against them. This was reported and the landlord's name was removed from the list. This wife also relates other experiences:

> I used to tell landlords that my husband is black, or if my husband made the contact, he would tell them I am white. When we first got married, we decided . . . actually he decided, that when we looked for housing it would be best to let people know we were an interracial couple. When I would make calls, I got such remarks as: "What do you mean by interracial? Do you mean you are Catholic?" My answer was no. Then another silly question was: "Do you mean man and woman?" I said: "Of course I mean that—mean my husband's black and I'm white." They would hang up the receiver and all sorts of things like that.

In order to avoid embarrassment and humiliation, some couples made telephone calls to inquire if landlords had any objection to renting to mixed couples. A third respondent reported that only in one instance did a landlord admit to his objection. On the other hand, although evidence is inconclusive, he strongly feels that in two other cases, racial discrimination was a factor in his not getting the dwelling.

In Lafayette, Indiana, after one of these families had looked at a house advertised for rent, the landlord, upon learning of their identity, told them it was no longer available. About two days later, the wife had a friend inquire about this same house, and strangely enough, it was available again. They made several calls to other places and asked if there were any objection to renting to an interracial couple. Among other negative responses, a few landlords replied with mutters about their other tenants' feelings and refused to rent to them.

It was also revealed that some landlords fit Merton's prejudice typology of prejudiced nondiscriminators and unprejudiced discriminators. For such people, there seems to be a lack of correspondence between attitudes and behavior.[8] Moreover, it appears that some individuals possess personality traits of both. For example, one respondent mentioned that one landlord was willing to rent to all-black or all-white couples, but not ones that were mixed.

A white Chicago engineer reported that "once you move into a place, it doesn't seem to make a difference as to how people feel." But yet, it sometimes does. Distressed to find a black living in their midst, some whites may become alarmed and sell their homes to black families, thereby launching population shifts which can change the whole structure of their communities.[9] Moreover, while interracial couples are prepared to experience initial resentment of their presence in white neighborhoods, it comes as a surprise to some of them, especially to the white partners, to find hostility in black communities as well.[10]

Although they are in the minority, a few families reported having no problems with renting housing in predominantly all-white communities. The present data suggest that resistance to desegregation of housing is much stronger than it is regarding jobs. On the other hand, in public apartment complexes in which a great number of tenants are students, younger couples, and transient populations, the housing issue appears not to be of great magnitude.

EMPLOYMENT

About three decades ago, Drake and Cayton observed that one of the primary difficulties of the mixed married is keeping a job. Both partners usually find or feel it necessary to conceal their marriage from white employers. Most of the couples interviewed talked rather freely about themselves, but when questions were raised concerning their employment, they were reluctant to give information. As one white wife put it: "We have to be careful because we are buying our home and can't afford to lose our jobs. If we had enough money to be independent, we wouldn't care who knew we were married."

A second woman who worked as a domestic for a white family recalled the pressure she was subjected to when her employer learned of her intent to marry a black man who worked for the same family:

> My employer saw the notice in the *Daily News*. He
> asked if it was true. I told him it was true. He said: "You
> are new here. You don't know what it's like here. Do you
> know what will happen if you marry this man? You will be
> ostracized. No one will want to have anything to do with
> you." I said: "I am going to do it." Then he said: "You
> have a friend in Texas. I'll get you a ticket and you can
> go there till it blows over." He tried to get me to go...
> but I didn't.

Drake and Cayton indicate that fear of economic reprisal
seemed least pronounced among civil service employees and independent entrepreneurs, with black physicians being best able
to escape economic reprisals.[11]

In the present investigation, a majority of the husbands
and wives are employed. Most of them work in semiprofes-
sional capacities. A small minority had been dismissed from
their jobs and pointed out that being interracially married is
a possible explanation. There are some difficulties in the area
of employment; however, they are not insurmountable. One
black husband explained that his marriage was certainly a factor in not being able to hold some jobs over a long period of
time:

> But then there are jobs I could have got but there are
> "brothers" who offer information to the white cat that runs
> the establishment ... like they will tell the man: "you don't
> want him because he married out of his race." You have
> "brothers" who look at me because I'm black in a white
> situation and say that I'm a traitor; but the same things that
> apply to them still apply to me no matter what situation
> I'm in.

Bruce (a second black groom) reported being dismissed
from jobs. In some cases, racial discrimination was difficult to
prove. But after an intensive investigation, he concluded that
his marriage must have been the only reason. Some white co-
workers who had previously maintained a cordial relationship
with him, after learning of his marriage, no longer did so.

A third black groom lost a good-paying job because of his relationship with a white female (later his wife) who worked for the same company. They had been secretly dating for quite some time. One day, for no apparent reason, he was told that his services were no longer needed. About two years later, a white male friend informed him that his interracial dating was the reason for his dismissal.

One bride who was teaching in a public school related being ousted from the system for a similar reason:

> They told me that I would work better in a ghetto rather than a regular situation. Because my husband was black, they didn't want him, or my child anywhere near.

A second wife lost a job. She relates this story:

> I was waiting tables for what some people call poor white trash. He was a Greek. When he found out my husband was black, he tried to date me himself. And when I didn't go out with him, he said: "Well, I'm going to have to let you go. I found out that you are married to a Negro." After that I went to work for a black man, who was a gambler. He hired me as a barmaid. He also rented us an apartment.

A third white bride, who works as a beautician, said her co-workers were shocked when they learned she was dating a black man. They told her to keep such personal affairs hidden for this would hurt their business if customers found out about it. The boss, who is foreign-born, expressed a similar view.

A fourth wife who had been working at a local bank as a secretary-receptionist for three years reported having problems. Two weeks after a new manager was hired, he found an excuse to fire her. The excuse was that one day she left the office for a few minutes without informing anyone as to her reason for being out. This wife explained that her new boss was extremely prejudiced and some of the bank's other officers also wanted to get rid of her. She explains:

> It was just something he drummed up. As long as my old boss was there, they couldn't touch me; because he had

told them I did good work; and that there was no reason to fire me. But the moment he resigned, that was it!

She has no doubt that the source of this "discriminatory action" was her marriage.

Sometimes discrimination works in reverse—i.e., blacks, especially females—might also express dissatisfaction with a white person who is married to a black. One of the white wives had worked for an Affirmative Action Program as a teacher of underprivileged people—who in this case were primarily black women. She taught clerical skills as well as other subjects to prepare them to pass a general examination for a certificate equivalent to a high school diploma. These black women expressed dissatisfaction in that they did not relate to their white teacher and vice versa. She was later replaced with a black person. This bride felt that her marriage was a factor in the action taken against her.

Some couples have not had unpleasant experiences in their occupations. For example, one husband commented:

> We have not had problems in getting and keeping a job. A job for my wife was no problem because I've known her employer for a very long time.

According to the wife:

> My employer has a habit of employing "misfits"— people who appear to be "off," or strange and who have a hard time trying to find work. He seems to have a lot of them working for him.

One black husband had not detected any negative reactions:

> It wasn't a big thing like everybody found out about it all at once. The workers gradually learned about it each in their own way. I might be driving down the street with my wife in the car, and see one of the fellows and honk my horn. She usually picks me up for lunch and after work; and in the course of the day, coming in and out of the place, they would see her and recognize the car. They figured she's been with me so many times, she must be my wife.

Upon being interviewed for a position at a local television station, a second black husband informed the management of his plans to marry a white girl; and if there were objection on the part of the company, he would prefer not to be considered for the job. He was told that his personal life did not matter to them. Their only concern was whether or not he could perform his duties efficiently. There was some question, however, about their having children:

> The station manager was rather concerned about the kind of children we would have...and what they would look like. He thought they might be spotted or checked, because wasn't that what the word "mulatto" meant? I assured him that it didn't mean that and showed him the definition in a dictionary...and now he doesn't worry.

This person is employed as a photographer-reporter. Moreover, the company employs three other men who are interracially married; two are black-white pairs, the other Oriental and white.

A second bride who works as a secretary reported having no repercussions on her job. The husband has attended her annual office Christmas party for two years, and nobody seems to think anything of it.

Whenever Ray (a white husband) was considered for jobs which required an interview, he always made it a point to take his wife along. He pointed out:

> Once I was a candidate for a position at one of the large computer companies. When the big "wheels" took me out for dinner and cocktails, I made sure that Susan was around. No one seemed bothered about it...so I felt she was accepted.

Generally speaking, a majority of the couples have had few problems regarding employment. I would venture to say that because of the impersonal nature that characterizes many work relationships in large-scale organizations, employers and supervisors are more concerned about the employees' efficiency than about their personal lives. Then too, out of a fear that someone might exert pressure, many employers are probably less willing to take the risk of dismissing a person solely on the basis of one being interracially married.

Blacks today as well as in the past have had limited economic and political control over service institutions in their own community. For example, there are few black-owned businesses; blacks do not employ a significant number of other blacks; housing, in a majority of the cases is rented or sold by whites; schools and hospitals are either controlled or owned by whites; and most policemen who have contacts with the black community are white. Because of these vast economic, political, and social inequities between blacks and whites, it is somewhat understandable why blacks are not treated as social equals. It is likely that if significant gains were made in the economic and political spheres of social life, there would be less aversion to black-white marriages by larger society.

RELATIONS WITH THE BLACK COMMUNITY

This section focuses attention on the positive, neutral, and negative reactions of friends, neighbors, and black women in the black community. As I pointed out earlier, until recently, the white partner in a black-white marriage was usually accepted in the black community. In fact, in the past a majority of those who contracted such marriages established residence in black neighborhoods. But currently, some blacks have indicated as much opposition to this phenomenon as have some whites. Irrespective of this opposition, ten couples reported being accepted by their black neighbors.

Positive Reactions

Several white wives indicated that after being rejected by the white community they had no place to turn except to their black friends. One bride is accepted by one of her black female neighbors as a daughter. Thus, she is proud of the close bond which exists between the two of them. Because of this rejection by the white community, for some of these brides, the black counterpart has served as a sanctuary. One mother compares their experiences in the two communities:

> When we lived in the ghetto about three years ago, our children ran the streets until 10 o'clock every night. We never had to worry about anything happening to them. We were inexpressibly happy. I have a bunch of little girls ... my yard was always full of everybody's children. I had tons of cookies and candy to give all of the kids. But since we moved into this white neighborhood, things are different. Now we are isolated.

The increasing development of black pride has no doubt altered many of the cordial views previously held by many blacks toward black-white marriages. Without a doubt, a large number of Afro-Americans now perceive other blacks who marry across racial lines as traitors to their race. This is thought to be completely inconsistent with a developing sense of black pride.

Neutral Reactions

Eight of the couples reported having no relationship with the black community. One white bride expressed the view that:

> We are more or less ignored by the blacks. Even though we live in this community, most of them will not associate with us. I don't think they care one way or the other. They stay to themselves and we to ours.

Another of the white wives stated that she hasn't lost any friends because she didn't have any in the beginning; and further indicates:

> The black women in this community do not accept me. I haven't really come in contact with the intelligent black women whom I believe would accept me. I only have two white girl friends. One is divorced; and the other is a German girl who was brought here by a Negro G.I. They are married; but it is kind of on the rocks ... because he keeps messing around with older black women.

From all indications, it appears that some blacks are simply indifferent toward mixed marriages. Their alleged manifestations of apathy might be attributed to this transitional stage of collective identification—i.e., black awareness. In all likelihood, this attitude will be pronounced for a while; but if the objectives of a black peoplehood are achieved, intermarriage may come to be accepted.

Negative Reactions

At one time a black man with a white woman was looked on with awe by other blacks because he was a taboo defier, "a player with lightning." Now, against the growth of black awareness, he is often criticized by his own race for making such a choice. However, some black men believe that racial interaction helps destroy racism and is therefore a justification for dating whites.[12] Despite this argument, black-white marriages are not accepted as much by blacks today as compared with a few years ago.

Some of the white spouses have recently noticed significant changes in the attitudes and reactions of blacks toward them. Most of the negative changes, however, are exhibited by black females and some older black couples. On the other hand, younger black males appear not to care one way or the other about mixed marriages.

One wife remembered when she was in high school, she was never uncomfortable around black people:

> I never felt that I had to say anything different than I would in front of whites. I just acted the way I was and never felt that I was being looked at as something different. But lately, I'd say in the last couple of years—and especially among young blacks—I feel extremely uncomfortable. I know that I am not accepted; I mean ... I've been told by black people that I am not accepted. I've been told: "Don't even bother coming around." And this is a new thing for me.
>
> Not too long ago, we went on campus to attend a meeting. And this girl said to me: "No! White people are not allowed in here." I told her that I was with my man,

and where he goes, I go also. This is a new thing for me. I never had to deal with it before; and I find it extremely difficult to handle. This puts me in a terrible position because now I have to revamp my entire thinking.

Reactions from Black Females

A growing number of black women are viewing with increasing concern, and, often hostility, the mounting competition from white women for eligible black males. Interracial dating and marrying are attacked as being incompatible with the concept of black identity.[13]

The *New York Times* observes that most of these women are young with a strong sense of identity and reject the melting pot concept. They say: (1) It is important that members of the black community remain united, but interracial relationships tend to militate against the unity; (2) black women are increasingly aware of their own worth, beauty, and ability to contribute to the future of their race; (3) there is a numerical preponderance of black women to black men; and (4) there is a substantially stronger feeling against black men dating white women, although most of the women who reject interracial dating and marriage think it should apply equally to both sexes.[14]

According to Bernard, the competition for mates among black women is intensified by the unwillingness of some men to marry at all. Many of the surplus black women will never marry unless they do so across racial lines. And a number of others will marry men whose educational and cultural standards may not be the same as their own. At least for some time to come, many black women cannot assume with any degree of confidence that they will be able to look to marriage for either economic or emotional support.[15]

One solution proposed by black psychiatrist Kermit Mehlinger is that black women borrow a leaf from the men's book and date white. Although a few would be willing to do so, it is unlikely that this suggestion will meet widespread acceptance. Most black women are solidly opposed to interracial dating, which they view as a contradiction for a true black person. As one woman put it: "I don't want to date a white guy . . . moreover, I have trouble understanding why black men want to date white women. Progress for us is going to have to start with the improvement of the black male-female relationship."[16]

SUMMARY

Despite the trend toward the elimination of discriminatory barriers and the amelioration of racial prejudice in America, generally speaking black-white marriages are still not accepted by a majority of whites. Evidence suggests, however, that an increasing number of people are becoming more receptive or at least tolerant of these marriages.

The present investigation indicates that a large number of blacks are also opposed to this marriage pattern. For example, many black females and older blacks are the most vehement opponents. The large national surplus of black women to black men may explain the loudest protest by the former. A black who dates or marries white is ostracized by some as a traitor to his or her race. However, others justify it on the basis that it helps to destroy racism. Younger black males tend to express apathy regarding these unions.

In regards to securing housing and employment, some gains have been made within the last two decades. These couples live in all type neighborhoods—with a slight majority in either all black or on the periphery of predominantly all white communities. Some are discriminated against in their efforts to obtain housing; some are not. Housing seems to be less of a problem if the wife is black. Some overt hostility toward mixed families exists in both black and white communities. The least amount appears in public apartment complexes.

A majority of these families have had no difficulties in the area of employment. However, a small number reported

8

Egalitarianism through Black Nationalism

MUCH SPECULATION AND some controversy center on the question of whether interracial dating and marriage are inimical to the successful development of a black peoplehood. Washington observes that black awareness is a two-edged sword,[1] in that it is a strategy designed to achieve complete social, economic, and political equality through the development of black identity and a sense of peoplehood. There appears, however, to be a relationship between intermarriage and the enhancement of one's social status. This chapter examines how a racial minority in this country might improve its social position through marital alliances with members of the dominant group. Attention is focused on: (1) perspectives on stratification, (2) economic inequality and intermarriage, (3) a comparison of miscegenation and race relations in Mexico and Brazil with those in the United States, (4) a theory of upward mobility for black Americans, and (5) equality through racial mixture.

PERSPECTIVES OF STRATIFICATION

Americans differ considerably in their work, educational, and leisure aspirations, to what types of people they accord prestige to and the amount of power they would like to exercise over others. But they differ much less on questions concerning the value of income and wealth. For it is precisely these two items that enable one to seek the amount and kind of education desired and, hence, the kind of occupation one might enter. Income and wealth set limits on the ways in which interests and lifestyles are expressed. Thus, as both Karl Marx and Max Weber have argued in slightly different ways, a person's economic standing is the keystone of his life; it literally determines his life chances. So again we are forced to return to income and wealth as the pivotal issues in the study of social inequality.[2]

According to Kingsley Davis and Wilbert E. Moore, "Social inequality is an unconsciously evolved device by which societies insure that the most important positions are conscientiously filled by the more qualified persons."[3] Melvin M. Tumin, however, points out that this argument for the necessity of social inequality runs into a number of theoretical and empirical difficulties. In looking at the real world, one can immediately see that people are not sifted and sorted into appropriate positions of privilege and disprivilege. In terms of social position, it is possible to move upward and downward, but the probabilities governing the end result are largely set from birth —in even the most open societies. Rather than some sort of meritocracy where every individual begins the "competition" from the same line, the starting blocks are so widely staggered that the runners in the rear have only a remote chance of catching up with those ahead, while those starting ahead must virtually quit to even begin to lose ground.[4] T. M. Bottomore asserts that a more accurate description of the social class system is that it operates largely through the inheritance of property, so as to ensure that each individual maintains a certain social position, which is determined by birth irrespective of particular abilities.[5]

There is no reason to assume that a direct relation exists between native abilities and material success, or in functional language, that "the most important positions are filled by the most qualified persons." Sociological critics of this view such as George Homans and Gerhard Lenski perceive other grounds of social inequality: the power of various individuals and groups to self-designate and command for themselves wealth and economic privilege (and, of course, to transmit and inherit it). In Homans' view, society does not reward people, but rather people and groups with scarce resources, increasingly artificially preserved and self-designed, garner what they can, owing precisely to the economic power derived from the scarcity. By restricting the supply of services and skills, even a society with the productive and individual capacity to provide unlimited abundance can persist in sharp stratification and inequality. Finally, as Homans points out, it is the scarcity that makes a person or group important, not some natural hierarchy of social importance.[6]

Moreover, Lenski contends that as a society's surplus increases so does inequality. Elites tend to accumulate the surplus wealth. However, Lenski argues that the direct relationship between surplus and inequality reverses itself in advanced industrial society as elites increasingly make concessions so as to avoid discontent in the rest of the society.[7] Charles H. Anderson comments, however, that Lenski seems to have confused the overall rise in the standard of living in advanced industrial society with a reduction in inequality and that presently there has been no such trend in the United States toward greater equality of wealth. The millionaires just become multimillionaires, and the multimillionaires become centimillionaires and even billionaires, while millions of persons live in starchy poverty.[8]

Despite the gradually shifting trends in the United States, vestiges of the old order continue to prevail. For example, the proportion of college graduates among young black adults had more than tripled between 1955 and the 1970s. But many found that their education did not make important differences. Their skin was still black. Employment open to them was still mostly in the menial and lower class jobs. Others discovered that even though their earning power was greater, there was still the problem of finding suitable housing and good schools for their children. A few selected blacks have been able to approach the American main stream. However, they run the risk of being alienated from the culture from which they came and are likely to remain on the edge of the culture they are seeking to enter. On the other hand, the masses of blacks are not feeling this change. With their wants and needs stimulated by the tantalizing hope that comes from seeing others break through and achieve, they escalate their discontent.[9]

An examination of the distribution of income in the American population shows glaring differences. Nonfarm families with incomes under $3,968 in 1971 were defined and specified by the United States Census Bureau as "poor," that is, unable to adequately provide food, clothing, shelter, education, health care, and other essentials for themselves. Yet 8.2 percent of white families and 29.7 percent of nonwhites (mainly blacks) had incomes that year under the minimum figures. Even more striking was the fact that 1.5 percent of all American families, involving over a million persons, had incomes under $1,000, scarcely sufficient for luxurious living. At the other end of the spectrum, over one-half of the white families and 30 percent of the nonwhites had incomes in excess of $10,000 in 1971.[10]

Cutting across the various levels of a class structure are such components as race, ethnicity, and religion, each adding to the complexity of the system. In American cities, racially visible minorities are distributed throughout the entire social structure, but most are concentrated on the lower levels. This is especially true of the black population. Although black and other racial minorities have generally moved up considerably in the economic structure in recent years, their relative positional change in the social system has been small or even nonexistent. Hence, the social and economic gap between them and the white majority has not been reduced much if at all because the whites have also moved upward in the economic system. Most urban blacks have been viewed by whites as lower class, partly because they are people against whom white prejudices are often directed, and partly because the white majority is reluctant to relinquish its position of privilege and prestige.[11]

ECONOMIC INEQUALITY AND INTERMARRIAGE

Since most of the income and wealth are either owned or controlled by whites, and not blacks, the important question here then is: Does a continually increasing number of black-white marriages necessarily decrease status differences between black and whites? To this question, many would answer in the affirmative. For example, Heer observes that the informal prohibitions on intermarriage serve to perpetuate the pattern of inequality because they make it unlikely for blacks to inherit wealth and other resources from whites. On the other hand, there are counterarguments. A case in point involves Jewish Americans. Although rates of intermarriage for this group are low, despite certain barriers, Jews have achieved an average socioeconomic position at least as high as the rest of the population.[12]

The major weakness in this analysis is that Jewish, unlike black Americans, do not have the skin color problem. It should also be kept in mind that an extremely high rate of intramarriage among Jews is by choice. But to what extent would this rate decrease if Jews decided not to remain so endogamous? It is well documented that white Americans are much less averse to intermarriage with white ethnics, despite a difference in religion or culture, than they are with racial ethnics and minorities—i.e., "people of color." Thus, from one perspective, it could be hypothesized that the strength of the link between low frequency of black-white marriage and the black man's inferior socioeconomic status is uncertain. But on the other hand, the skin color problem might make a world of difference. For without a doubt, it impedes marriage between blacks and whites which preclude the blacks from inheriting income and wealth from the whites.

Washington points out that to assume the black-white issue to be a class problem is to have faith that it will fade away when blacks experience greater economic gains. It is a dream to hold that the problem can continuously be evaded by pushing education, jobs, and legal relief in the expectation that the rise of blacks in the economic sphere will eliminate the sharp conflict implicit in the low incidence of black-white marriage. The issue is not only economic but also full acceptance of blacks and their exercise of freedom of choice which would also allow whites the same privilege. The problem is nothing less than one of social exclusion.[13]

In those cultures where the custom or law prohibits exclusion of minority group members from important societal spheres, relations between the majority and minorities, indeed take on a different blend. Two classical examples of how racial patterns vary from those of the United States are provided by Mexico and Brazil. An examination of this phenomenon in both countries follows.

MEXICO

Of all the multiracial societies created by the expansion of Europe since the late fifteenth century, interestingly enough those of Spanish America stand out as exhibiting only traces of the racist virus. This is true not only in predominantly white countries such as Argentina, Chile, and Uruguay but also in Bolivia, Ecuador, Peru, and Guatemala where Indians still comprise 40 to 45 percent of the population. The same holds true for Venezuela and Cuba with their strong African admixtures. Moreover, racial characteristics have little social relevance in modern Mexico. The complex interplay of race and culture through the dual process of miscegenation and hispanicization have so homogenized the Mexican population that race and ethnic relations in that country have received only scant attention from social scientists. Let us take a further look at the factors that account for this situation.

Hispanicization and Mestization

The exploitative conquest of the Spanish colonial government over Mexico was accompanied by two continuing processes that dominated Mexican history: (a) hispanicization, that is, the partly coerced, partly voluntary adoption of the colonial version of Spanish culture by the indigenous and African population; and (b) mestization, that is, the genetic mixture of the three main human stocks present in New Spain—the African, the European, and the Indian. Culturally, modern Mexico is a mixture of indigenous and nonindigenous elements, but the Spanish component is clearly dominant. Biologically, the reverse is true; the Indian contribution to the national gene pool continues to dominate.

The term *mestizo*, originally a racial one used to designate the mixture of European and Indian, has now acquired a cultural meaning and is applied to practically anybody who is not of recent European origin and who speaks the Mexican dialect of Spanish as his mother tongue. Over 85 percent of today's population of the republic fall in this category. For example, "pure" Indian declined from 98.7 percent of the total in 1570 to 74.6 percent in 1646, to 60 percent in 1810, to an estimated 20 percent in 1950. The mestizos increased correspondingly to something like four-fifths of the modern Mexican population. Most individuals of predominantly pure Indian stock have become more or less completely hispanicized, so much so that the racial definition of mestizo or Indian has now lost its meaning.

It should be pointed out that despite the widespread miscegenation which occurred in Mexico, colonial New Spain, from the early seventeenth century to independence, was stratified into five distinct groups called called *castas*. These were defined by a mixture of racial and cultural characteristics and could more accurately be described as estates rather than castas. But the continuing process of hispanicization and miscegenation increasingly blurred the dividing lines and made for considerable upward mobility—though much less than in an open class system.

If the Spaniards exhibited a clear form of racism, it was toward people of African descent. Indians were considered not as noble as the Spaniards, but neither were they considered intrinsically ignoble. They were in need of enlightenment through exposure to the true faith, but they were basically human. Spanish attitudes toward blacks were distinctly different. Africans were regarded as a vile, immoral race possessing unclean blood and low intelligence. But at the same time they were considered to have muscular strength and endurance, manual dexterity, and high fertility.

The Role of the Catholic Church

In spite of these highly derogatory attitudes toward blacks and mulattoes, slavery in Mexico was less brutal than in the English colonies, largely as a result of the tempering influence of the Catholic Church. Although the Catholic Church was the empire's largest landowner and greatest exploiter of peoples in Mexico, it did play a humanizing and universalistic role in the area of race. Church prelates put a stop to the enslavement of Indians and mitigated that of Africans. The church refused to accept the validity of racial distinctions. Behind every face, no matter how swarthy, it found a soul to save, by force if necessary.

As a result, the rigidity of the colonial caste system was being undermined during the eighteenth century by increasing mestization and hispanicization, the slow economic demise of slavery, and the absorption of blacks and mulattoes into the Indian and mestizo population. The War of Independence, much like the American Revolution, did not profoundly affect the economic and social structure of Mexico. The gradual physical and cultural homogenization which had begun in the sixteenth century was perhaps slightly accelerated through political independence.

Mexico then can be described as having evolved from a paternalistic type of race and ethnic relations to a nonracial system without having gone through a competitive phase. In other words, race ceased to be a meaningful social reality and ethnicity was relegated to a residual position as the quasifeudal colonial society broke down and gave rise to a modern class society. How did the concept of race fade out of Mexican social reality?

A common answer to this question is that racism never really existed in Mexico because it was alien to Spanish culture. It is true that Iberian racism was milder and quite different from the crude Northern European nineteenth-century variety. In Spain and Portugal the indigenous population had been ruled until the fifteenth century by the Moors who were both darker skinned and more educated than the natives. Hence, the Spaniards in the Old World did not associate dark skin with political or cultural inferiority; to say, however, that racism was unknown in Iberian culture, particularly in the New World, is an untenable overstatement. Physical traits were used to categorize people in colonial times; the elaborate racial terminology is symptomatic enough of concern for race; in addition, the frequent use of such phrases as "pure race," "clean blood," and "suspicious color" in colonial documents testify to the existence of Iberian racism. Having thus established the historical existence of the phenomenon, how does one account for its subsequent disappearance?

Several lines of explanation are suggested. First, the Spaniards seldom made a clear analytical distinction between race and culture. Rather, they tended to assume that the two went together, and their alleged cultural superiority has always been a greater source of pride to them than the "purity" of their physical makeup.

Second, few of the invidious distinctions and discriminations prevailing during colonial times followed a strictly racial line. To virtually all rules, norms, and caste-linked disabilities there were important exceptions. There are, for example, recorded cases of intermarriage between Spaniards and both Indians and Negroes. Laxity often prevailed in recording a person's caste in baptismal or census records. So gradually, the ostensibly racial classification finally became quite flexible and bore only an approximate relationship to genetic reality which in turn was further facilitated by the continuing and parallel processes of hispanicization and mestization. This contributed significantly to a blurring of both ethnic and racial distinctions.

Finally, the concern for physical appearance and its consequent elaborate taxonomy of racial pher otypes militated against the drawing of rigid color lines. The minutia with which shades of color were distinguished and the complexity of a terminology which reserved a special term for every possible crossing of Indian, European, and African over at least three generations greatly lowered the reliability and validity of classification. By the time of independence the social validity of these terms was practically nil, and racial labeling was little more than a narcissistic salon game for bored aristocrats and erudite pedants. The system broke down under the weight of its own complexity and thus favored rather than hindered racial mobility. Mexico had indeed become a nation of bronze.

BRAZIL

When Pedro Alvares Cabral sighted Brazil in 1500, Portugal claimed it as hers, but it was not until 1532 that an effective colonial government was established and that regular contact between the two countries was initiated.[14] Wherever the Portuguese went—to Africa, India, China, or to the New World—they mixed with the native peoples. Gilberto Freyre has shown, Portugal itself in the sixteenth century was a country of mixed racial backgrounds. As pointed out in the Brazilian case (with the Spaniards), since the dark Mohammedan Moors, who also dominated Portugal, brought a superior culture with them to the New World, the Portuguese, just as the Spaniards, did not identify dark skin with a subjugated "inferior" people.[15]

Since Brazil as a political unit was a creation of the Portuguese, the traditional patterns of government, administration, business enterprise, law, and education are derived from Portugal. Although American influences are strong in one region of the country, African influences in another, and recent northern European influences in still another, it was the Portuguese who were the governors, and in a broad sense, the teachers of Brazil during the period of formation of the national culture. The Portuguese, in a sense, are the common denominator of all Brazil.

With the relative lack of racial antagonism in Brazil, mixture between the three racial stocks (whites, blacks, and Indians) has occurred with unusual frequency. There are mixtures of every conceivable degree, as well as combinations of these three basic stocks. Only among the descendants of the old aristocracy do people claim pure Caucasian descent and even these "old families" speak with pride of a distant Indian ancestor.

The Impact of Culture on Status

As elsewhere, slavery was a brutal institution in Brazil but even during slavery, the Negro and mulatto gained a place in Brazilian life far superior to that of dark people in the British and Dutch colonies to the north. In the British colonies, freedom of the Negro did not give him the rights of a citizen. By contrast, in Brazil the mulatto and the freed Negro were granted the rights of citizens and took part in public life. Moreover, as in Mexico, the tolerance of the Portuguese owners in Brazil toward a people of darker skin was strengthened by the position of the Catholic Church, which considered the slave to be the moral equal of the master.[16]

Carl N. Degler notes that it is often said that the much longer experience of the Portuguese with dark-skinned people is an important part of any explanation as to why there has been little acute racial antagonism between the two groups. It is true that the Portuguese confronted Africans two centuries or more before Englishmen had any contact with them in any numbers in North America. For the Portuguese expansion into Africa began in 1415, whereas the first Negroes did not come to Jamestown until 1619, and then in small numbers. But despite the suggestiveness of the argument from time, it is misleading. Time in itself does nothing. What counts is what goes on during the passage of time. For example, there may be minor differences in the attitude and behavior of white Georgians or South Carolinians toward blacks in 1790 as compared with 1940, but they are unimportant. In both periods whites consistently treated blacks as inferior. Yet during that century and a half, whites and blacks lived, loved, worked, and died side by side. Near proximity over four or five generations did almost nothing to alter the relationship between the races for during that time the full weight of the society was directed toward maintaining white supremacy. On the other hand, in a mere twenty-five years since 1950, integrational events and circumstances have done more to weaken the idea and the practice of white supremacy than ten times that number of previous years, even if the idea and practice have still not been totally eliminated. Put in such concrete terms, the proposition that the mere passage of time brings change is obviously inadequate. What then makes for a sharp variation in the attitudes toward race and color in the two countries?

The "Mulatto Escape Hatch"

According to Degler, a profound example that unlocks the puzzle of the differences in race relations in Brazil and the United States is the "mulatto escape hatch." Complex and varied as race relations in the two countries have been and are today, the presence of a separate place for the mulatto in Brazil and its absence in the United States nevertheless defines remarkably well the heart of the difference.

The existence of an accepted status for the mulatto in Brazil, for example, makes most difficult, if not impossible, the kind of segregation patterns that have been so characteristic of the United States. With many shades of skin color, segregating people on the basis of color would involve both enormous expense and great inconvenience. Public facilities, for instance, would have to be duplicated several times, beyond reason and financial feasibility. Furthermore, in a society in which distinctions are made among a variety of colors, rather than by race as in the United States, families would be split by the color line. Children of mulattoes, after all, vary noticeably in color. In view of the high value that Western society places upon the nuclear family it would be neither practical nor likely that a system of segregation disruptive to families would be permitted to develop. Moreover, in a society in which the mulatto has a special place, a racist defense of slavery or of Negro inferiority cannot easily develop, for how can one think consistently of a white or a Negro race when the lines are blurred by the mulatto? The search for purity of race is thus frustrated before it begins. Similarly, the existence of the "mulatto escape hatch" helps to explain why relations between the races in Brazil have been less rigid and less prone to hostility than in the United States. The presence of the mulatto not only spreads people of color through the society but it literally blurs and thereby softens the line between black and white.[17]

The "mulatto escape hatch," however, only explains a dimension of the complex and varied racial patterns in Brazil. It is far from being the solution to race problems in that country. Other influences that explain the marked differences in race relations between Brazil and the United States are: (1) the Portuguese culture itself, (2) the attitude of the Catholic Church, (3) the relatively lenient laws that governed slaves, and (4) the slow and careful policy used to liberate slaves after 1800. These cultural elements are significantly different from those regarding race relations in the United States. These examples are not intended to convey the idea that Mexico and Brazil are free of racial prejudice and discrimination. This is far from the truth. They merely suggest that the intensity of racial tensions in these two cultures are much milder than in the United States. But in this country, how would one go about trying to create a racial climate that even approximates the ones just described? One of the most obvious problems is that the black struggle in America lacks a theoretical model by which to bring about this condition.

A Theory of Upward Mobility for Blacks

Solomon P. Gethers notes that one of the biggest problems of the current Black Power Movement is that it lacks a consistent ideology or theory of social change. To develop such a theory, the contemporary movement must be examined within the context of the entire historical struggle for freedom. For instance, what can be said about the relationship between the Black Power Movement and the Civil Rights Movement? Between the Black Power Movement and the Black Muslim Movement? Are we dealing with alternative approaches to a common problem? In what ways do the various approaches conflict? Are the goals of each separate, distinct, and diametrically opposed or integral parts of a larger design?[18] To begin to answer these and similar questions calls for the type of historical analysis advocated by Harold Cruse. He indicates that the radical wing of the Negro movement in America sorely needs a social theory based on the living ingredients of Afro-American history. Without such a model, all talk of black power is meaningless.[19]

Neither black power nor civil rights (securing citizenship rights) alone provides a complete explanation of the Afro-American liberation struggle. These are but two of five major social movements that have taken place among black Americans during the last 160 years. The others are (1) the Tuskegee self-help program (economic self-sufficiency), (2) the Black Muslim Movement and (3) the Marcus Garvey Back-to-Africa Movement (the quest for ethnic self-determination). Gethers takes the position that these five constitute the core of an historical process directed toward the ultimate liberation of Afro-Americans.

In this connection, E. Franklin Frazier (1968) makes an important distinction between integration and assimilation. Integration, he says, is defined as the acceptance of the individual Negro into the economic and social organization of American life; whereas assimilation is said to lead to "complete identification with the people and culture of the community in which the social heritage of different people become merged or fused." Integration is only the first stage in the solution of still a larger problem which involves not only individuals but also the organized life of the black community vis-a-vis the white community.[20]

In short, the emphasis on integration and assimilation in the Civil Rights Movement has led to systematic debasement of the social heritage and the creative potential of the black community. Frazier, in 1955, and Harold Cruse almost five years later, hold the so-called black intellectual responsible for this unhappy situation.

The point is, liberation for the black man simply cannot take place in the absence of a positive sense of black ethnic selfhood. By the same token, ethnic selfhood alone is not sufficient. It is a mutually interdependent part of the single historical process. The liberation of Afro-Americans does not and cannot depend on any one strategy alone, but on the achievement of all three in a yet to be understood time phase and pattern of articulation.

In the past, goals, strategies, and tactics in the movement have been generally worked out in a blind and uncritical manner. What is required at this juncture is a carefully developed ideology by which immediate and long range plans can be systematically fashioned. However, strategy employed at any one stage should be selected and developed in relationship not only to the immediate objectives of that stage but to the total historical process.[21] In this connection, Farber's notion of "symbolic estates" and related assumptions generates much understanding about the dynamics of social processes and mobility patterns in contemporary urban-industrial societies. As a model for upward mobility for black Americans, it is suggested that an ordered set of theoretical constructs be grounded in this concept.

Symbolic Estates and a Black Peoplehood

Farber observes that societies which emphasize kinship as a means of sustaining social differentiation appear to organize distinct kin groups on the basis of lineage segments. Possibly the most valuable property of a lineage segment is its position among other kinship groups in terms of honor and status, a position defined by the content of the symbolic estate that the kinship group possesses. This symbolic estate includes the achievements and honor of both living and dead relatives (real or fictional). The role of *kinship groups* in social differentiation may be regarded as the perpetuation and enhancement of these symbolic estates.[22]

A basic characteristic of *descent groups* is that they provide for the inheritance of relatives as well as physical property. The living and deceased relatives of ego's descent group give to the individual an identity in terms of his historical roots and status in the world around him. The inheritance of relatives thereby serves to symbolize the individual's place in the scheme of things.[23]

The content of symbolic family estates seems to (a) motivate individuals toward achievement, and (b) provide them with a conceptual scheme of social organization signifying the importance of status in interaction as well as economic resources to achieve their aspirations. In the absence of such estates, functionally equivalent substitutes can be developed. For example, in recent years, the concept of black peoplehood has developed among black Americans. It is perhaps significant that this group has adopted this conceptualization in an attempt to develop cohesiveness in a hostile world. The development of black peoplehood as an analogue to symbolic family estates suggests that comparable efforts are being made to establish symbolic estates among this segment of the lumpenproletariat.[24]

I agree with Farber's conception of the role of the kinship group in social stratification and would add a corollary: In this era, the black community can function as a quasikin group and be regarded as the perpetuator and enhancer of its symbolic estate—i.e., black awareness. This idea explains how a black peoplehood might facilitate the achievement of more freedom and equality, which then, would likely result in more numbers of blacks and whites being eligible for marriage with anyone willing to enter into such a contract. One of the basic ingredients involved in the development of a peoplehood concerns an individual's sense of pride, self-respect, and positive self-image. These are personality traits that many black Americans have been unable to acquire.

A Developing Sense of Identity

Slavery was so shattering an institution that the traditional culture of Afro-Americans was completely lost. Their cumulative experience with others has led to a negative self-image.[25] "For what if there is nothing," asks Erik Erikson, "in the generation past nor in the accessible resources of the contemporary community which would help to overcome the negative image held up to a minority." What indeed? This is the crux of the identity problem when there is a past to live down and; worse still, it is difficult to prevent the future from being premised on that past.[26]

The models for personal beauty in America have been white, as have been all other cultural standards. Black people had no choice but to measure themselves, to some extent at least, by those standards. It has been impossible for blacks not to fall victim to this white assessment of themselves, while at the same time resisting it. Under the influence of Malcolm X and Elijah Muhammad, and with the coming of black power, blacks began both to rediscover and recreate an identity. However, much is involved in the symbolic return to black roots. It is, above all, a way of coming to terms with the past in a present whose history still shows in its social structure. Blacks cannot escape the past until they accept it.[27]

Black Americans suffer from many problems of identity and negative self-image. The Civil Rights Movement has generated some changes but integration as presently practiced does not seem to offer the masses a solution to problems of negative self-concept. It has been suggested by Alvin F. Poussaint that token integration into white institutions may lead to even greater identity crises for Afro-Americans.

Black consciousness movements appear to be able to contribute a great deal to blacks' sense of identity and self-esteem, and could mobilize the black community for positive political and social action. The development of black consciousness (symbolic estates) also serves as an alternative and supplementary approach to the building of blacks' self-image along with the present drive toward complete racial integration.[28]

There is now talk of "soul," suggestive of a subculture. Until recently there have been lower-class adaptations to the fact that the dominant goals that are accepted cannot be attained. The function of soul then is to idealize the accomplishments of the lower class and to proclaim the superiority of its way of life. Self-doubts are eased as the soul brothers reassure themselves of their success since having "soul" is superior to having anything else. Convinced of their own worth, they thereby belong to a select group rather than to a residual category—surplus population.[29]

The rhetoric of soul is reinforced by such symbols as food and music and dress to express the ideals and avoid the realities of lower-class life in the black ghetto. It does not add up to a culture, yet there is something in it that serves as a source of self-respect. Soul is a social style, a way of presenting the self to others, rather than a way of life, but a style that is black, not white.[30]

The rise to the surface of black consciousness would seem to be a most powerful refutation of black-white marriages as a resolution of black subordination. Black consciousness, given the American experience, is absolutely inevitable, indispensable, and necessary for the freedom of blacks and whites. It is not sufficient, however. Black consciousness is the process whereby American blacks become indelibly impressed with the

fact that they are descendants of slaves and continue to be cap-
tives without freedom, justice, and equality. This historical
perspective and present awareness both provide the urgency
for a truly integrated society; and at the same time, the de-
mand for the resources and freedom to develop a separate black
community as a viable option for blacks who wish it.[31]

The rapid rise of race pride in this century which culmi-
nated in the Civil Rights Movement suggests that blacks believed that the American Creed will overcome. Therefore no
black leader has found it expedient to support miscegenation.
This tactic was obviously a political necessity in order to gain
the indispensable cooperation of whites, so blacks had no alternative but to accept the antiassimilation ideology. To assume that blacks have not advocated intermarriage because a
majority of whites dislike the idea is to mistake practicality for
causation.[32]

Equality Through Racial Mixture

Many of the couples interviewed in this study feel that
the only way American society can ameliorate the problem of
prejudice and racism is through intermarriage. As one respondent puts it: "If there were no blacks or white, but everybody
was a mixture of the two, this would be a much better country
in which to live." Some of the black males, precisely advanced
this reason for "crossing the racial line." In a similar vein,
Danny K. Davis argues that:

> If this country is going to survive, we have to try to rid it
> of the myths and phobias that one race might have about
> the other. The best way to do this, is through all kinds of
> interaction, including interracial marriage.

Black psychiatrist Mehlinger also suggests that the only
thing different about an interracial marriage is that racism
adds complications to the routines of married life. Many of
these unions are much healthier than the so-called "homogamous" ones. For it usually takes a person with strong character

structure to go into such a relationship in the first place. More-over, Mehlinger does not feel that interracial dating or mar-riage is weakening the process of black identity. He sees it in-stead as a strengthening factor.[33]

Gordon Allport also suggests without a doubt that lifting the sexual ban would reduce the glamour and conflict between blacks and whites. The central question allegedly then is inter-marriage. The fact that miscegenation between two healthy people has no weakening effect on the offspring is overlooked. Intermarriage cannot rationally be opposed on biological grounds. It can, however, be opposed on the ground of the handicap and conflict it could cause both parents and offspring in the present state of society.

For the most part then, the basis for the argument against interracial marriage is invalid and irrational. It comprises a fierce fusion of sex attraction, sex repression, guilt, status su-periority, occupational advantage, and anxiety. It is because intermarriage would symbolize the abolition of prejudice and economic and class barriers that it is so strenuously fought.[34]

The gradual integration of minority groups into the main stream of American life has increased contact between groups and is therefore decreasing the social and economic obstacles which previously separated them. Racial prejudice has also been publicly defined as illegitimate. It is likely then that all types of mixed marriages will continue to increase in the near future. But there is still much opposition to intermarriage. For in the product of such union, racism sees its own destruction.

Many whites no doubt will continue to exploit the fear of black-white marriage as a means of retaining economic domi-nance, and as a devastating question to be raised in connec-tion with any concessions which might be made by blacks. It is necessary, then, that blacks devise an ordered set of theoretical constructs under which a strategy to attack racism can be de-veloped. The notion of a "symbolic family estate" might achieve this end. Black awareness will have some negative effect on the rate of black-white marriages, but it is my guess, that if there is a decrease, it will be slight and only for a short period of time. One reason is that through the development of a "symbolic family estate," blacks will increasingly achieve a higher status. For it is only through the achievement and the realization of this complete selfhood can the black man exercise greater control of his destiny.

Future black-white marriages will have a more congenial climate for success as society continues to become more attuned to individual freedom and personal rights regardless of race, color, creed, or religion. Social scientists can also play a vital role in improving conditions (for the interracially married) by objectively analyzing this phenomenon so that many of the myths, misconceptions, and underlying principles of failure are put to rest. Such studies, would not necessarily facilitate an increase in interracial marriages, but would certainly provide a healthier climate for those who choose to enter such a relationship.

Black-white marriage then should have a tremendous impact upon race relations in the United States. It is relatively unimportant as to whether the incidence of these alliances increase or remain the same, but it is of much concern to many individuals that these unions are approved by a larger society. It is my conviction that the degree of acceptance of this phenomenon is one of the most accurate indices for measuring the extent to which a group is achieving social, economic, and political equality. If complete acceptance comes to pass, it is likely that discrimination in the United States, based on race or skin color will cease to exist.

chapter notes

1 Perspectives on Black-White Intermixture

1. Edward B. Reuter, *Race Mixture: Studies in Intermarriage and Miscegenation* (New York: McGraw-Hill, 1931), pp. 27–30.
2. This information is cited in Lerone Bennett, Jr.'s *Before the Mayflower: A History of Black America* (Chicago: Johnson Publishing Co., 1969), p. 244, which is based largely on James Hugo Johnston's doctoral dissertation at the University of Chicago, "Race Relations in Virginia and Miscegenation in the South, 1776–1860," Carter G. Woodson's article, "The Beginnings of the Miscegenation of the Whites and Blacks" in the *Journal of Negro History* III (October 1918), and A. W. Calhoun's study, *A Social History of the American Family*, 3 vols. (Cleveland: Clark, 1917).
3. Edward B. Reuter, *The Mulatto in the United States* (Boston: Gorham Press, 1918), p. 106.
4. Ibid., p. 11.
5. Ibid., p. 106.
6. Charles F. Marden and Gladys Meyer, *Minorities in American Society* (New York: D. Van Nostrand, 1973), p. 148.
7. George E. Simpson and J. Milton Yinger, *Racial and Cultural Minorities: An Analysis of Prejudice and Discrimination* (New York: Harper and Row, 1965), p. 279.
8. Marden and Meyer, *Minorities in American Society*, p. 150.
9. Robert S. Stuckert, "The African Ancestry of the White American Population," *Ohio Journal of Science* 55 (May 1985): 155–160.

10. Simpson and Yinger, *Racial and Cultural Minorities: An Analysis of Prejudice and Discrimination,* p. 380.
11. These ideas are based upon Bennett's *Before the Mayflower: A History of Black America,* pp. 249–258.
12. John H. Franklin, *From Slavery to Freedom: A History of Negro Americans* (New York: Alfred A. Knopf, 1967), p. 225.
13. Bennett, *Before the Mayflower: A History of Black America,* p. 244.
14. This section is based on data from Reuter's *Race Mixture: Studies in Intermarriage and Miscegenation,* pp. 78–103.
15. Bernard Farber, *Family and Kinship in Modern Society* (Glenview, Illinois: Scott, Foresman, 1973), pp. 36–37.
16. Reuter, *Race Mixture: Studies in Intermarriage and Miscegenation,* p. 103.
17. Cloyte M. Larsson, *Marriage Across the Color Line* (New York: Lancer Books, 1965), p. 38.
18. Bennett, *Before the Mayflower: A History of Black America,* pp. 263–265.
19. Richard H. Klemer, *Marriage and Family Relationships* (New York: Harper and Row, 1970), pp. 110–112.
20. Lloyd Saxon, *The Individual, Marriage, and the Family* (Belmont, California: Wadsworth, 1968), p. 330.
21. J. Ross Eshleman, *The Family: An Introduction* (Boston: Allyn and Bacon, 1974), p. 312.
22. Sophia F. McDowell, "Black-White Intermarriage in the United States," *International Journal of Sociology of the Family* 1 (May 1971): 49–58.
23. Robert O. Blood, Jr. *Marriage* (New York: Free Press, 1969), p. 95.
24. Gunnar Myrdal, *An American Dilemma* (New York: McGraw-Hill, 1964), pp. 60–61.
25. Emory S. Bogardus, *Immigration and Race Attitudes* (Boston: D. C. Heath, 1928), p. 25.
26. Brewton Berry, *Race and Ethnic Relations* (Boston: Houghton Mifflin, 1965), p. 289.
27. Robert K. Merton, "Intermarriage and the Social Structure: Fact and Theory," *Psychiatry* 4 (August 1941): 361–374, in Rose L. Coser, ed. *The Family: Its Structure and Functions* (New York: St. Martin's, 1964), p. 128.
28. Ibid., p. 132.
29. Eshleman, *The Family: An Introduction,* pp. 280–281.
30. Merton, "Intermarriage and the Social Structure: Fact and Theory," pp. 140–141.
31. Eshleman, *The Family: An Introduction,* p. 280.

32. Bernard Barber, *Social Stratification* (New York: Harcourt, Brace, 1957), p. 123.
33. Kingsley Davis, "Intermarriage in Caste Societies," *American Anthropologist* 43 (July-September 1941): 388–395, in Rose L. Coser, ed. *The Family: Its Structure and Functions* (New York: St. Martin's 1964), pp. 106–108.
34. Robin Fox, *Kinship and Marriage* (Baltimore: Penguin, 1967), p. 235.
35. Claude Lévi-Strauss, *The Elementary Structures of Kinship* (Boston: Beacon, 1969), p. 479.
36. Farber, "Affinity and Descent in Industrial Societies," *The Journal of Comparative Family Studies.* 3 (Spring 1972): 125–147.
37. Farber, *Kinship and Class: A Midwestern Study* (New York: Basic Books, 1971), p. 12.
38. Fox, *Kinship and Marriage,* p. 228.
39. Ibid., pp. 218–219.
40. Farber, *Kinship and Class: A Midwestern Study,* pp. 12–14.
41. David M. Heer, "Negro-White Marriages in the United States," *Journal of Marriage and the Family* 27 (August 1966): 262–273.
42. Fox, *Kinship and Marriage,* pp. 238–239.
43. Farber, *Family: Organization and Interaction* (San Francisco: Chandler, 1964), pp. 105–110.
44. Ibid., pp. 151–153.

2 Incidence and Nature of Black-White Marriages

1. Sophia F. McDowell, "Black and White Intermarriage in the United States," *International Journal of Sociology of the Family* 1 (May 1971): 49–58.
2. National Center for Health Statistics *Vital Statistics of the United States, 1970,* Volume II, Marriage and Divorce (Washington, D. C.: Government Printing Office, 1970).
3. J. Ross Eshleman, *The Family: An Introduction* (Boston: Allyn and Bacon, 1974), p. 314.
4. Louis Wirth and Herbert Goldhamer, "The Hybrid and the Problem of Miscegenation," in Otto Klineberg, ed. *Characteristics of the American Negro* (New York: Harper and Row, 1944), p. 276.
5. Paul H. Jacobson, *American Marriage and Divorce* (New York: Holt, Rinehart, and Winston, 1959), p. 62.
6. Thomas P. Monahan, "Interracial Marriage in the United

States: Some Data on Upstate New York," *International Journal of Sociology of the Family,* 9 (March 1971) : 94–105.

7. John H. Burma, "Interethnic Marriage in Los Angeles, 1948–1959," *Social Forces* 42 (December 1963) : 156–165.

8. David M. Heer, "Negro-White Marriages in the United States," *Journal of Marriage and the Family* 27 (August 1966): 262–273.

9. Thomas P. Monahan, "Interracial Marriage and Divorce in the State of Hawaii," *Eugenics Quarterly* 13 (March 1966) : 40–47.

10. Cloyte M. Larsson, *Marriage Across the Color Line* (New York: Lancer Books, 1965) , p. 37.

11. Heer, "Negro-White Marriages in the United States," pp. 262–273.

12. Henry A. Bowman, *Marriage for Moderns* (New York: McGraw-Hill, 1965) , p. 297.

13. Carl N. Degler, *Neither Black Nor White* (New York: MacMillan, 1971) , p. 268.

14. Bowman, *Marriage for Moderns,* p. 207.

15. Heer, "Negro-White Marriages in the United States," pp. 262–273.

16. "Boy, Girl, Black, White," *Time,* 16 June 1970, p. 74.

17. Bert N. Adams, *The American Family: A Sociological Interpretation* (Chicago: Markham, 1971) , p. 226.

18. Loving v. Commonwealth of Virginia, 338 U. S. 1, 87 S. Ct. 1817 (1967) .

19. Eshleman, *The Family: An Introduction,* p. 313.

20. Loving v. Commonwealth of Virginia, 338 U. S. 1, 87 S. Ct. 1817 (1967).

21. Bernard Farber, *Family and Kinship in Modern Society* (Glenview, Illinois: Scott, Foresman, 1973) , p. 37.

22. Joseph R. Washington, *Marriage in Black and White* (Boston: Beacon Press, 1970) , p. 149.

23. Edward B. Reuter, *The Mulatto in the United States,* (Boston: Gorham Press, 1918) , pp. 135–136.

24. W. E. B. Dubois, *The Philadelphia Negro: A Social Study* (New York: Schocken, 1967) , pp. 358–367.

25. Ray E. Baber, "A Study of 325 Mixed Marriages," *American Sociological Review* 2 (October 1937) : pp. 705–716.

26. Wirth and Goldhamer, "The Hybrid and the Problem of Miscegenation," pp. 276–277.

27. Reuter, *The Mulatto in the United States,* pp. 136–137.

28. Dubois, *The Philadelphia Negro: A Social Study,* 1967, p. 362.

29. Baber, "A Study of 325 Mixed Marriages," pp. 705–716.

30. Dubois, *The Philadelphia Negro: A Social Study,* pp. 364–365.

31. Wirth and Goldhamer, "The Hybrid and the Problem of Miscegenation," pp. 249–370.
32. St. Clair Drake and Horace Cayton, *Black Metropolis* (New York: Harcourt, Brace, and World, 1945), pp. 138–141.
33. Joseph Golden, "Characteristics of the Negro-White Intermarried in Philadelphia," *American Sociological Review* 19 (April 1953): 144–147; and "Social Control of Negro-White Intermarriage," *Phylon* 20 (February 1958): 273–284.
34. Larry D. Barnett, "Interracial Marriage in California," *Marriage and Family Living* 25 (November 1963): 424–427.
35. Kingsley Davis, "Intermarriage in Caste Societies," *American Anthropologist* 43 (July-September 1941): 388–395, in Rose L. Coser, ed. *The Family: Its Structure and Functions* (New York: St. Martin's, 1964), pp. 106–108.
36. Wirth and Goldhamer, "The Hybrid and the Problem of Miscegenation," pp. 249–370.
37. E. Franklin Frazier, *Black Bourgeoisie* (New York: Free Press, 1962).
38. Todd H. Pavela, "An Exploratory Study of Negro-White Intermarriage in Indiana," *Marriage and Family Living* 26 (May 1964): 209–211.
39. Jessie Bernard, "Notes on Educational Homogamy in Negro-White and White-Negro Marriages," *Journal of Marriage and the Family* 27 (August 1966): 274–276.
40. Albert I. Gordon, *Intermarriage* (Boston: Beacon Press, 1964), pp. 316–334.
41. John Dollard, *Caste and Class in a Southern Town* (New York: Doubleday, 1949), pp. 156–157.
42. Baber, "A Study of 325 Mixed Marriages," p. 158.
43. Drake and Cayton, *Black Metropolis,* pp. 141–159.
44. Golden, "Characteristics of the Negro-White Intermarried in Philadelphia," pp. 144–147; and "Social Control of Negro-White Intermarriage," pp. 273–284.
45. Charles E. Smith, "Negro-White Intermarriage: Forbidden Sexual Union," *Journal of Sex Research* 2 (November 1966): 169–177.
46. Gordon, *Intermarriage,* p. 348; and N. Weyl, *The Negro in American Civilization* (Washington: Public Affairs Press, 1960).
47. Dubois, *The Philadelphia Negro: A Social Study,* pp. 358–367.
48. Baber, "A Study of 325 Mixed Marriages," pp. 705–716.
49. Wirth and Goldhamer, "The Hybrid and the Problem of Miscegenation," pp. 249–370.
50. Harold T. Christensen, *Marriage Analysis: Foundations for*

Successful Family Life (New York: Ronald, 1958), p. 287.

51. Thomas P. Monahan, "Intermarriage and Divorce in the State of Hawaii," *Eugenics Quarterly* 13 (March 1966): 40–47.

52. William M. Kephart, *The Family, Society, and the Individual* (Boston: Houghton Mifflin, 1961), p. 607.

53. Thomas P. Monahan, "Are Interracial Marriages Really Less Stable?" *Social Forces* 48 (June 1970): 461–473.

54. Golden, "Characteristics of the Negro-White Intermarried in Philadelphia," pp. 144–147.

55. Larsson, *Marriage Across the Color Line,* pp. 69–71.

3   Methodology and Data

1. U. S. Department of Commerce, Bureau of the Census, *General Population Characteristics: 1970,* PC (1)-B15, p. 103.

2. Bernard Farber, *Kinship and Class: A Midwestern Study* (New York: Basic Books, 1971), p. 3.

3. U. S. Department of Commerce, Bureau of the Census, *General Population Characteristics: 1970,* PC (1)-37, p. 157.

4. U. S. Department of Commerce, Bureau of the Census, *General Social and Economic Characteristics: 1970,* PC (1)-C2, p. 157.

5. *Encyclopaedia Britannica,* 15th ed.

6. U. S. Department of Commerce, Bureau of the Census, *General Population Characteristics: 1970,* PC (1)-B26, p. 55.

7. *Encyclopaedia Britannica,* 15th ed.

8. Albert I. Gordon, *Intermarriage* (Boston: Beacon, 1964), pp. 1–2.

9. William M. Kephart, *The Family, Society, and the Individual* (Boston: Houghton Mifflin, 1972), p. 296.

10. Joseph Golden, "Characteristics of the Negro-White Intermarried in Philadelphia," *American Sociological Review,* 19 (April 1953): 144–147.

11. John H. Burma, "Interethnic Marriage in Los Angeles, 1948–1959," *Social Forces* 42 (December 1963): 156–165.

12. Todd H. Pavela, "An Exploratory of Negro-White Intermarriage in Indiana," *Marriage and Family Living* 26 (May 1964): 209–211.

13. Norman K. Denzin, *The Research Act: A Theoretical Introduction to Sociological Methods* (Chicago: Aldine, 1970), p. 141.

14. George H. Mead, *Mind, Self, and Society* (Chicago: University of Chicago Press, 1937), p. 7.

4 Motives for Black-White Marriages

1. Robert K. Merton, "Intermarriage and the Social Structure: Fact and Theory," *Psychiatry* 4 (August 1941): 361–374 in Rose L. Coser, ed., *The Family: Its Structure and Functions* (New York: St. Martin's, 1964), p. 145.
2. John A. Osmundsen, "Doctor Discusses Mixed Marriages" *New York Times,* 7 November 1965, p. 731.
3. Lloyd Saxton, *The Individual, Marriage and the Family* (Belmont, California: Wadsworth, 1968), p. 332.
4. Ruth S. Cavan, *The American Family* (New York: Thomas Y. Crowell, 1969), p. 206.
5. Bert N. Adams, *The American Family* (Chicago: Markham, 1971), p. 229.
6. Cavan, *The American Family,* p. 206.
7. Saxton, *The Individual, Marriage and the Family,* p. 332.
8. Richard L. Rubenstein, "Intermarriage and Conversion on the American College Campus," in Werner J. Cahnman, ed., *Intermarriage and Jewish Life* (New York: Herzl, 1963), pp. 122–142.
9. Saxton, *The Individual, Marriage and the Family,* pp. 332–333.
10. Robert O. Blood, *Marriage* (New York: Free Press, 1969), p. 95.
11. Bernard Farber, *Family: Organization and Interaction* (San Francisco: Chandler, 1964), p. 122.
12. Ibid., p. 152.
13. William H. Grier and Price M. Cobbs, *Black Rage* (New York: Basic Books, 1968), p. 92.
14. Elridge Cleaver, *Soul on Ice* (New York: Dell, 1968), p. 14.
15. Grier and Cobbs, *Black Rage,* pp. 91–92.
16. Jean Carey Bond and Pat Peery, "Has the Black Man Been Castrated?" in Robert Staples, ed. *The Black Family: Essays and Studies* (Belmont, California: Wadsworth, 1971), pp. 141–143.
17. John H. Bracey, Jr., August Meier, and Elliot Rudwick, *Black Matriarchy: Myth or Reality?* (Belmont, California: Wadsworth, 1971), p. 1.
18. Robert Staples, "The Myth of the Black Matriarchy," in Robert Staples, ed., *The Black Family: Essays and Studies* (Belmont, Calif.: Wadsworth, 1971), pp. 150–151.
19. Abram Kardiner and Lionel Ovesey, *Mark of Oppression* (Cleveland: World Publishing Co., 1962), p. 70.
20. Bond and Peery, "Has the Black Man Been Castrated?" p. 141.
21. Joan Downs, "Black/White Dating," *Life* (May 28, 1971): pp. 56–67.

22. Bond and Peery, "Has the Black Man Been Castrated?," pp. 141–143.
23. Everett V. Stonequist, *The Marginal Man* (New York: Charles Scribner's Sons, 1937), p. 3.
24. Downs, "Black/White Dating," pp. 56–67.

5   Black-White Marital Combinations

1. U.S. Department of Health, Education, and Welfare, "Marriages: Trends and Characteristics," United States, Series 21 (September 1971), p. 20.
2. J. Ross Eshleman, *The Family: An Introduction* (Boston: Allyn and Bacon, 1974), p. 316.
3. Robert K. Merton, "Intermarriage and the Social Structure: Fact and Theory," *Psychiatry* 4 (August 1941): 361–374 in Rose L. Coser, ed. *The Family: Its Structure and Functions* (New York: St. Martin's, 1964), pp. 133–150.
4. Kingsley Davis, "Intermarriage in Caste Society," *American Anthropologist* 43 (July-September 1941): 338–395.
5. Bert N. Adams, *The American Family* (Chicago: Markham, 1971), p. 228.
6. Merton, "Intermarriage and the Social Structure: Fact and Theory," pp. 150–151.
7. Adams, *The American Family*, pp. 228–229.
8. Eshleman, *The Family: An Introduction*, p. 216.
9. Louis F. Carter, "Racial Caste Hypogamy: A Sociological Myth?" *Phylon* 29 (Winter 1968): 347–350.
10. Louis Wirth and Herbert Goldhamer, "The Hybrid and the Problem of Miscegenation," in Otto Klineberg, ed. *Characteristics of the American Negro* (New York: Harper and Row, 1944), p. 282.
11. Paul H. Jacobson, *American Marriage and Divorce*. (New York: Holt, Rinehart, and Winston, 1959), p. 62.
12. U.S. Department of Commerce, Bureau of the Census, *United States Census of Population: 1960, Subject Report, Marital Status,* Report P.C. (2) -4E, p. 160.
13. Jacobson, *American Marriage and Divorce*, p. 62.
14. U.S. Department of Commerce, Bureau of the Census, U.S. *Census of Population: 1960, Subject Report, Marital Status,* Report PC (2)-4E, pp. 160–161.
15. U.S. Department of Commerce, Bureau of the Census, *United States Census of Population: 1970, Subject Report, Marital Status,* Report PC (2), pp. 262–263.

16. Davis, "Intermarriage in Caste Societies," *American Anthropologist,* pp. 388–395.
17. Glenn H. Elder, Jr., "Appearance and Education in Marriage Mobility," *American Sociological Review* 34 (August 1969): 519–533.
18. J. Richard Udry, Karl E. Bauman, and Charles Chase, "Skin Color, Status, and Mate Selection," *American Journal of Sociology* 76 (January 1971): 722–733.
19. William C. Kvaraceus, et al., *Negro Self-Concept: Implications for School and Citizenship* (New York: McGraw-Hill, 1969), p. 43.
20. Bernard Farber, *Family: Organization and Interaction* (San Francisco: Chandler), chapters 4 and 5.

6 Dating, Weddings, and Marital Relations

1. Ruth S. Cavan, *The American Family* (New York: Thomas Y. Crowell, 1969), p. 208.
2. St. Clair Drake and Horace Cayton, *Black Metropolis* (New York: Harcourt, Brace, and World, 1945), p. 133.
3. Joan Downs, "Black/White Dating," *Life* 70 (May 28, 1971): 56–67.
4. Ibid.
5. Ibid.
6. Frank A. Petroni, "Teen-age Interracial Dating," *Transaction* 8 (September 1971), pp. 54–59.
7. Cloyte M. Larsson, *Marriage Across the Color Line* (New York: Lancer Books, 1965), p. 60.
8. Joseph R. Washington, *Marriage in Black and White* (Boston: Beacon Press, 1970), p. 220.
9. Ibid., p. 295.
10. Albert I. Gordon, *Intermarriage* (Boston: Beacon Press, 1964), pp. 322–326.
11. William H. Whyte, Jr., *The Organization Man* (New York: Simon and Schuster, 1956), pp. 378–379.
12. Washington, *Marriage in Black and White,* p. 296.
13. Ibid.

7 Relations with the Larger Community

1. Rosalind Wolf, "Self-Image of the White Member of an Interracial Couple," in Jacqueline P. Wiseman, ed. *People as Partners* (San Francisco: Canfield Press, 1971), p. 58.

2. Cloyte M. Larsson, *Marriage Across the Color Line* (New York: Lancer Books, 1965), p. 55.
3. Ibid., pp. 55–56.
4. Ibid., p. 57.
5. Ibid., p. 56.
6. Ibid., p. 57.
7. Ibid., pp. 56–57.
8. Brewton Berry, *Race and Ethnic Relations* (Boston: Houghton Mifflin, 1965), pp. 301–302.
9. Larsson, *Marriage Across the Color Line*, p. 57.
10. Ibid., p. 56.
11. St. Clair Drake and Horace Cayton, *Black Metropolis* (New York: Harcourt, Brace and World, 1945), pp. 136–141.
12. Joan Downs, "Black/White Dating," *Life* 70 (May 28, 1971): 56–67.
13. Danny K. Davis, "Sister Debates a Brother on That Black Man/White Woman Thing," *Ebony* 25 (August 1970): 130–133.
14. Enid Nemy, "Numbers of Black Women Say They Will Not Date White Men," *New York Times* (November 23, 1970): 44c.
15. Jessie Bernard, *Marriage and Family Among Negroes* (Englewood Cliffs, New Jersey: Prentice-Hall, 1966), p. 84.
16. Downs, "Black/White Dating," pp. 56–67.

8   Egalitarianism through Black Nationalism

1. Joseph R. Washington, *Marriage in Black and White* (Boston: Beacon Press, 1970), p. 25.
2. Charles H. Anderson, *Toward A New Sociology: A Critical View* (Homewood, Illinois: Dorsey Press, 1971), pp. 83–84.
3. Kingsley Davis and Wilbert E. Moore, "Some Principles of Stratification," *American Sociological Review* 10 (April 1945): 242–249.
4. Anderson, *Toward A New Sociology: A Critical View*, p. 85.
5. T. M. Bottomore, *Classes in Modern Society* (New York: Vintage Books, 1968), p. 11.
6. George Homans, *The Nature of Social Science* (New York: Harbinger Books, 1967), pp. 66–68; and Gerhard Lenski, *Power and Privilege: A Theory of Social Stratification* (New York: McGraw-Hill, 1966).
7. Lenski, *Power and Privilege*, p. 315.
8. Anderson, *Toward A New Sociology: A Critical View*, pp. 88–89.

9. Charles W. Fisher, *Minorities, Civil Rights, and Protest* (Belmont, Calif.: Dickenson, 1970), p. 19.
10. Noel P. Gist and Sylvia F. Fava, *Urban Society* (New York: Thomas Y. Crowell, 1974), pp. 330–331.
11. Ibid., p. 332.
12. Heer, "Negro-White Marriages in the United States," pp. 262–273.
13. Washington, *Marriage in Black and White*, pp. 2–3.
14. Pierre L. van den Berghe, *Race and Racism: A Comparative Perspective* (New York: John Wiley and Sons, 1967), pp. 42–60.
15. Gilberto Freyre, *The Masters and Slaves* (New York: Alfred A. Knopf, 1946), pp. 185–278.
16. Charles Wagley, "Brazil," in Ralph Linton, ed., *Most of the World* (New York: Columbia University Press, 1949), pp. 213–270.
17. Carl N. Degler, *Neither Black Nor White* (New York: Macmillan, 1971), pp. 223–225.
    1971), pp. 223–225.
18. Solomon P. Gethers, "Black Nationalism and Human Liberation," *Black Scholar* 7 (May 1970): 65–73.
19. Harold Cruse, *The Crisis of the Negro Intellectual* (New York: William Morrow, 1967), p. 557.
20. E. Franklin Frazier, "The Failure of the Negro Intellectual," in *E. Franklin Frazier on Race Relations* (Chicago: University of Chicago Press, 1968).
21. Gethers, "Black Nationalism and Human Liberation," pp. 65–73.
22. Bernard Farber, *Comparative Kinship Systems* (New York: John Wiley and Sons, 1968), p. 10.
23. Farber, *Kinship and Class: A Midwestern Study*, p. 99.
24. Ibid., pp. 179–180.
25. Kenneth Clark, *Dark Ghetto* (New York: Harper Torchbooks, 1965), pp. 19–20.
26. Erik H. Erikson, *Identity: Youth and Crisis* (New York: Norton, 1968), p. 303.
27. Piri Thomas, *Down These Mean Streets* (New York: Signet Book, 1968), p. 123.
28. Alvin F. Poussaint, "A Negro Psychiatrist Explains the Negro Psyche," pp. 15–25 in Robert V. Guthrie (ed.), *Being Black: Psychological-Sociological Dilemmas* (San Francisco: Canfield Press, 1970).

29. Ulf Hannerz, "What Negroes Mean by Soul," *Trans-Action* 8 (July-August 1968) : 59–60.
30. David Wellman, "The Wrong Way to Find Jobs for Negroes," *Trans-Action* 5 (April 1968): 10–15.
31. Washington, *Marriage in Black and White,* p. 25.
32. Ibid., p. 12.
33. Danny K. Davis, "Sister Debates a Brother on That Black Man/ White Woman Thing," *Ebony* 25 (August 1970) : 130–133.
34. Gordon Allport, *The Nature of Prejudice* (New York: Doubleday, 1954), p. 354.

author index

subject index